Nine Months of Kindness

By Denise M. Baran-Unland

Cover art by Rebekah Baran

FIRST THOUGHTS

I had the idea for this book shortly after the 2019 WriteOn Joliet anthology release party in November (I am a co-founder and co-leader of WriteOn Joliet, an adult critique group).

Two of my goals prompted the concept. One is lofty, the other pragmatic.

Pragmatism first.

I wanted to produce a book that was more saleable than my fiction (I'm the author of most of the phantasmic fiction in the BryonySeries) in order to raise funds to market said fiction.

But also, I was ending the calendar year on a really grumpy note. For many decades, I've worked many long hours. But during the past few years, the hours have gradually increased until they overtook my life with no end in sight.

I really didn't like grouchiness creeping into my spirit, especially since I love my work. But in 2019, the work left little time for off-the-clock creative projects, which, believe it or not, makes me more effective at my "real" work.

I didn't want a different job. But I did want a different attitude.

So I decided to seek out tangible and practical ways in the midst of daily chaos to bless someone else and to notice and appreciate when people did the same for me.

My initial plan was to write an entry a day for 365 days. But an entry a day meant no published book until early 2021, and I wanted a book to sell at the 2020 anthology release party, a book that customers could give as a gift or use for themselves in 2021.

See? Pragmatic.

They say it takes twenty-one days to make a habit. But as the mother of many, I know it takes nine months to grow a fully developed baby.

For daily kindness to take root and live in my life, it needed time to fully mature. Hence, nine months.

Denise M. Baran-Unland
December 31, 2019

SECOND THOUGHTS

What a year 2020 turned out to be!

When I embarked on this journey/project, I hadn't envisioned a worldwide pandemic, never thought about facemasks, and "social distance" was an unfamiliar term.

In 2019, kindness was associated with closeness. In 2020, the kinder act was staying away – while seeking out creative ways to develop or maintain connection during the separation.

I'm certain 2020 has changed many of us in ways that are palpable and permanent.

But as long as that change means we've become more innovative in finding ways show kindness to others and more determined to root out unkindness in our lives, we can look back on 2020 with gratitude for the opportunities it gave us and look ahead to 2021 for more of the same.

Denise M. Baran-Unland
December 27, 2020

JANUARY 1, 2020

Be kind: Start a new year relieving the picky burdens of others.

Today is my last day of vacation; tomorrow I return to work.

I had a few last to-do items on my list: unpacking the three boxes that had sat beside my desk since we moved in October, finish reading Visage (I only made it halfway); and pruning my AOL account (over 2,000 unread emails in the last month, got to none of them).

The house also needed to be cleaned. Daniel's girlfriend Cindy was spending the weekend, and Rebekah was at work. I decided to let some of my personal projects go to tackle most of the house myself so everyone else could relax.

Daniel could spend time with his girlfriend, who lives out of town. And Rebekah could be spared one more task after a long day of her feet.

Don't get me wrong. I feel everyone should pitch in. And most of the time, they do. In fact, Cindy emptied and reloaded the dishwasher, and Daniel vacuumed the stairs and scooped the cat litter.

But there's also nothing wrong with occasionally doing it all to relieve someone else of the burden.

So I did.

JANUARY 2, 2020

Be kind: Recognize and meet a need.

My WriteOn Joliet co-leader Tom Hernandez called last night.

He had double-booked himself and could not make this night's meeting; should we cancel it?

It was my first day back to work; should I fly solo?

It's had been a few weeks since we'd had a regular meeting. I knew members would have pieces, and writing goals for the calendar year, they'd want to share.

So, no, I did not wish to cancel.

It's been a while since I've read one of my pieces, early September, I think. It's not that I don't bring a piece.

But the mother of six children and three stepchildren that still lives inside me wants to ensure everyone who brought a piece will read it and get the feedback they need to hear.

So I usually make a silent resolution to myself that I will wait until the end if there's time. Otherwise, I'll go "next time."

Tonight, everyone read but me. And I'm content.

I know what my reading sounds like. I write and edit for a living. I often hear feedback on my work.

This is why I can, and should, wait. And let someone else have the turn.

So I did.

JANUARY 3, 2020

Be kind: Set aside your own convenience for a cat.

We never set out to have a bunch of cats.

We took in our first stray, Frances, in October of 2005. She was about nine months old (the vet said). She came to the back door; Daniel fed her a can of tuna while I was upstairs in my attic office on an interview; and we wound up keeping and spaying someone's cat (We learned she'd been a stray for weeks, despite her red collar with the little jingle bell).

Next was Midnight, who came to us with ear mites and tapeworms when she was sixteen weeks old, a stray my oldest son Christopher had rescued.

Until she was tapeworm-free, the vet would not spay her. At nine months, still passing worm segments, she sneaked out of the house, and well...

My husband Ron named her kittens Faith, Hope, and Charity and refused to part with them. Charity used up all nine of his lives while we still had the house in Channahon; he is buried behind the garage with our dog Scooter.

Hope has been "temporarily" living with a family in Morris for five years. Faith and Frances live with us. Midnight lives with Timothy and attends kitty daycare at our house while he is at work.

Midnight likes to be held and petted A LOT and will cry for it A LOT. She sheds even more. I am allergic to cats, so I try to schedule long petting shortly before my shower.

She was crying like her heart was breaking when I walked into the house from work. She stayed at my heels, crying.

Finally, I donned my robe (to protect my clothes) and gave her a thirty-minute petting. When I was done, I had enough fur on that robe to make a coat, and I had more fur stuck to my face than was on Midnight (an exaggeration-ish).

We ended it sooner than Midnight wished. But she did stroll away content and not crying.

JANUARY 4, 2020

Be kind: Can you do it faster, better? Give the gift of time.

Today while my friend Sue (who is also one of my BryonySeries artists and a member of WriteOn Joliet), my youngest daughter Rebekah and I were finishing up our scroll art projects at Sue's house, Sue expressed her concern for another member of our group, a devout Christian, who is going through a deep depression following the closing of his church.

Sue suggested putting a care package together for him, and I suggested some "soul care" items, as well, similar to the items she put together in a little tin the Christmas before last, such as Bible verses to encourage him.

My comment reminded Sue of something. She excused herself from the room and soon returned with a bottle of tightly packed yellow-orange construction paper strips. Each strip has a Bible verse written on it.

Until I'd mentioned the verse, Sue had forgotten she'd owned this bottle. She'd had it a long time; even the cap was missing.

Sue started to read through a few strips, but she reads slower than I do, and the task was going to take her a long time and pull her away from the art scroll she was creating.

So I offered to read through the strips, probably a hundred in all, setting aside the encouraging ones I thought our friend might like.

Then I carefully stacked the other strips together and carefully returned them to the bottle.

This little act of kindness seems as inconsequential as taking a few minutes later that night to run the dishwasher, sweep the kitchen floor and around the little boxes, and wipe down the stove, all of which I did at midnight when I was getting ready for bed.

But reading the scrolls saved Sue lots of time. And adding those finishing touches in the kitchen made a pleasanter morning for Rebekah and Daniel.

JANUARY 5, 2020

Be kind: Show lots of support in simple acts.

We celebrate our family Christmas on January 7, which is also Rebekah's birthday.

Because of work schedules, available funds, and because we like sales, we did one day of Christmas shopping: today.

Rebekah is fighting either a mild flu or a bad cold. So when we got home, I made a big deal of making sure she could relax while I prepared dinner, which we ate together while we watched, and made fun of, the next episode of "Outlander."

But simple acts of support aren't one way in our family. For instance, while we were out shopping, Rebekah bought me a plush llama, which reminded me of my Larry the Llama character in several of my books in The Adventure of Cornell Dyer chapter book series.

And she also keeps a sharp eye on my clothing, noting when a seam is unraveling (which she stitches) or when items need dry cleaning (Rebekah takes them, picks them up, and, in some cases, pays for the cleaning), and replaces my nighttime "footies" with new soft plush ones when the old ones become worn and full of holes.

Small acts, much love.

But they create large amounts of love.

JANUARY 6

Be kind: Just fifteen minutes makes a difference.

Decades ago, I decided to become healthy. Part of my routine, in addition to striving for walking ten miles a day (or 23,000 steps) is to alternate nights of yoga and lifting light weights.

I come close to walking, especially since I do some of my work on my feet (like answering emails, social media, making phone calls), but my yoga and weight goas were harder to meet for many reasons: too tired, run out of time, extra work, etc.

Finally, I changed up those routines to fifteen minutes a night, with the goal of hitting five nights a week.

When I'm too tired, I remind myself it's only fifteen minutes. I can do fifteen minutes.

When I run out of time, I remind myself it's only fifteen minutes. It will not really impact getting the housework done or getting to bed on time.

Such a tiny amount doesn't seem like much. But because the workouts are consistent, I've noticed increases in flexibility and definition.

Most random acts of kindness take even less. Think of how many can be accomplished in fifteen minutes!

JANUARY 7, 2020

Be kind: Give the gift of grunt work.

Today we celebrated Christmas at my house. In attendance was five of the six children, all of the spouses and girlfriends except two, and all of the grandchildren except one.

Rebekah, who was still sick, had one request for her birthday: she did not want to cook.

She and one of my sons, Timothy, work in the culinary industry. For the past several years, they've taken over most of the traditional cooking at holiday meals because, quite frankly, they're better and faster at it.

I'm woefully out of practice. I haven't cooked much since 2008, when I handed off long research papers and the household chores to my home-schooled high schoolers and secluded myself to work and write my first novel.

We lost our home in early 2013 and had no kitchen for nearly a year so our eating became grazing, what we could pack into lunch boxes.

But a recent move into a larger townhome stirred feelings of homelife, and we've, I've, begun to gradually return to cooking.

So I did, in fact, cook most of the dinner by myself. I cleaned up a lot (not all) of it, so others could enjoy each other's company.

At our house, we tend to divide up grunt work and work together to get it done.

But sometimes, it's nice to shoulder it all, cheerfully and with love.

JANUARY 8, 2020

Be kind: Goodbyes can hurt. Be kind when you say yours.

Today my supervisor told me to shut down a social media group page that, a few years ago, I was told to start and grow in numbers and engagement.

But with new projects on the horizon, the company has decided to eliminate the group.

Shortly after I started the page, I greeted members with a friendly "good morning" and a photo of a cup of coffee.

The number of people who respond and greet each other good morning has increased.

So on the group's last official page, I posted the usual post with the message that the group was going away and expressing gratitude for the respectful posts and supportive community.

The number of comments amazed me.

A few had questions, which provided an opportunity for thoughtful answers and an opportunity to promote other groups where they might find a home.

A few had disparaging remarks, which provided an opportunity to uphold the company's decision and my support of it.

Most people expressed sadness and disappointment, which provided an opportunity for me to move those coffee posts to my personal page and invite people to connect with me there if they wished to continue it.

Takeaway: if you must part from another, do so gently.
It's the final memory you'll leave. Make it a good one.

JANUARY 9, 2020

Be kind: A new boundary brings new benefits.

A new salary law for 2020 meant I made the switch from salary to hourly, which is a bit of adjustment for me.

I'm not a clock-watcher, except in terms of meeting deadlines.

The nature of my work means the hours I work won't fit into a rigid template of time, such as 9 a.m. to 5 p.m.

But it does mean I'm not allowed to extend beyond a certain total of hours worked each week.

So although I always worked ahead early in the week to be ready for later in the week, when page counts were higher, I had to tighten that organization to make it fit into my new hourly status.

And since I'm receiving either new or modified job duties in a week or so, I also sharpened my priorities on what to accomplish, what to push back, what to let go.

I often laugh and say, "My lists have lists."

Over the last year, the list of undone items have grown.

Both my supervisor and HR have said the new law will benefit me.

The first benefit is the line drawn in the sand in terms of hours of time, which I must not cross.

It's changing how I plan.

It's making a healthy dent in my backed-up personal lists.

I'm beginning to remember what weekends look like.

We tend to rebel against rules.

But sometimes rules lighten our loads, giving us more time to lighten the loads of others.

JANUARY 10, 2020

Be kind: The healing power of coffee, tea, and conversation

Now that my Friday nights have returned, I made a coffee and book date with Sue.

Except the drizzle outside was supposed to turn into freezing rain as the night went on.

So when Sue arrived at our house, looking very tired, I proposed we just hang out at the house. She seemed reluctant but agreed.

I made tea for her and coffee for me. We talked a little about her books, even less about mine, and let the conversation run where it would for several hours.

As we talked, Sue became more awake, more animated, and, when the weather turned angry, and she decided to leave, more energized than I'd seen her all night.

As I wrote yesterday, we tend to rebel against rules.

But sometimes rules lighten our loads, giving us more time to lighten the loads of others.

First load lightened, check!

JANUARY 11, 2020

Be kind: You can't really be kind if you're not kind to yourself.

On January 15, 2014, my writing career changed its status, from freelance to employee.

Up until that point, I usually had several screens open during the day, so my muse was free to chase rabbit trails as they appeared.

I met my deadlines with my features writing. I met my deadlines with my children's schoolwork.

But because I freelanced, I could also refine a scene or a character or a piece of dialogue in the current novel-in-progress when inspiration struck.

When I became an employee, I moved any and all fiction to the weekend. I wouldn't even carry my fiction flash drive in my laptop anymore.

This made writing fiction challenging. I no longer could act upon creative lightning bolts. My muse needed time to walk up; I needed time to reengage with the story when Saturday arrived.

All of these ate into actual writing times.

As my work duties increased, my weekends decreased until they all but disappeared in 2019.

My muse was so tired, I could crank out very little fiction. To write imaginatively, one needs time for the imagination to play.

So during my vacation time over the Christmas and New Year's holidays, I did lots of nothing and tackled projects that didn't require much mental discipline.

Remember my personal to-do list? I shoved it to the side today and ignored its clamors for attention.

I have two novels in progress right now, and I felt wisps of creativity return.

Today, I was kind to myself. I drank some really nice dark roast coffee and let my muse play.

Be kind: Know your own needs; give to those who give to you.

Today Tom and I met with the deputy director at the Joliet Public Library to plan out 2020.

Last fall, the library reached out to WriteOn Joliet to form a partnership.

The library has been more than kind with ideas to help market us. But Tom and I balanced that with our ideas to help the library, too.

It's hard for writers to find readers, and the challenge is especially for writers who are local and self-published. Too often, artists think only about their own promotion, not how they can promote the promoter.

But partnerships are like any relationship. To be mutually satisfying, they must be mutually beneficial.

The library does not owe me or any other writer in our group a single thing.

But when it asked us, "How can we help?" Tom and I were prepared; we didn't waste the library's time. We had ideas, and the library had resources we had never considered.

And then it was our turn to ask, "How can we help you?"

It's not just marriages that require each partner to consider the needs of the other.

Be kind: A kindness shared is a kindness gained.

One of my cats Faith, a calico, is very squirmy when anyone pets her.

About a year ago, I trained her to like pets.

Faith is also VERY focused on routine. She likes meals, petting, really everything about her day to run on clockwork.

So I've also trained her to accept delays in meals and bedtime cuddling.

The problem is that, sometimes, I wind up nodding off before I give her the attention she needs.

And sometimes, another cat, Frances, claims the bed. Frances and Faith don't like each other, so if Frances gets to my bed first, Faith curls up on my desk chair.

This means, several nights can go by without Faith receiving any affection.

But on this particular night, when I was already late getting to bed, Faith was lying on the cat blanket on the end, eyes half-mast and resolved that tonight was not the night, either.

So instead of crawling under the covers, I lay down next to her and gave her a few gentle pats. Her eyes opened in surprise as if to say, "Really? We're really going to do this?"

She was on her feet in seconds, purring and making little chirruping noises as she twisted this way and that, her way of indicating the places she wanted to be petted.

After a long time, she settled back on the blanket, making sure her tail was touching my arm. Every now and then, she gave it a little flicker.

I felt super relaxed, too, and slept very well that night.

JANUARY 14, 2020

Be kind: A detour in your day might mean the world to another.

Even though I'm figuring out my old job in a new schedule, I picked up an extra story today.

It's an update on a story I wrote last summer, about a young mother with two young children who has stage 4 metastatic breast cancer.

I really only wanted to schedule an update. But the woman's sister wanted to talk to me right away, so I made some time for it.

Then I was going to wait to write the story because of my own limited time.

But I was concerned with the seriousness of the illness and the immediacy of her needs.

I'm not sure how I did, but I managed to get it written then and scheduled it for the following Tuesday, the best I could do.

It wasn't the workday I had planned.

But this young woman isn't having the life she had planned, and she may have less of it left than even her revised plans allow.

By next week, I won't even remember how or what I juggled to make this work.

But my efforts to inform the community and, perhaps, encourage them to help, will mean a lot to the family.

Be kind: Sometimes, the best show of appreciation is to show up.

Today is my six-year work anniversary with Shaw Media, which currently owns The Herald-News, where I am the publication's features writer/editor.

My company lets its employees take a vacation day in the month in which they were hired. Up until this year, I've always taken the fifteenth.

This year, I used January 7 (our family Christmas) and went to work on January 15.

I did this for two reasons.

In the past, I worked January 1 in order to take January 7 off. But as an hourly employee, I wasn't certain I could make the switch.

The second reason is that I'm very thankful for this job, not just because it's a job, but because I spend my work hours writing some really amazing, interesting, or inspiring stories.

Over my writing years spanning back to 1998, I've seen more features editors and writers go than I've seen arrive.

On my first day on the job, I knew I was no more indispensable than they were and that, one day, I too, might be a "go."

When so many newspapers have shut down, and when so many journalists no longer work in journalism, it is no small blessing to be working for the one publication in the world you wanted to work, writing the type of stories you want to write.

I felt the kind thing to do was to show up to work on the very day I was hired to do so, six years ago.

JANUARY 16, 2020

Be kind: Remember why people have two ears and one mouth.

Tonight was the second meeting of WriteOn Joliet for 2020. We meet twice a month.

I hung back with my piece until the end and actually read this time.

Mostly, I spent time listening carefully to pieces and offering thoughtful feedback from time to time.

Yes, many of the writers are hungry for feedback.

But being a writer, I know writers really want their audience to be hearers of their words.

So tonight, with my hours at work already lessened this month, and with my mind less fatigued, I was able to give that gift tonight, the gift of careful, reflective listening.

JANUARY 17, 2020

Be kind: Be the warmth in a winter storm.

I couldn't believe it when I clocked out. I was done for three days! Fiction!

The weather outside was frightful! But my inspiration was delightful!

But first, I talked to my mother, who lives out of state. And then I talked to my daughter, who lives out of state.

And then my son, who lives next door and was preparing for a food demo in another city tomorrow morning, rushed over in the snowstorm to have me look at his hand, which had a cat scratch and an injured finger, where he'd gotten it stuck in the door.

Both the scratch and the injury were deep. Yep! Quick care.

I offered to accompany him. Timothy, also being kind, felt the storm was too brutal. But I'm a mom. I went.

Even notice how driving snow feels like tiny razors against your face?

Quick care was just a few blocks away. We didn't wait too long. He had an X-ray; antibiotics were prescribed.

Timothy caught up on work email; I researched book marketing.

Soon, we headed back outside to drive to the pharmacy. We braved the elements, talked about whatever, braved the elements, waited for the medications to be filled, braved the elements, and then we were home.

Yes, Timothy is a grown man (twenty-nine) and did not need his mother to go with him to quick care. But that isn't the point.

While we were gone, Rebekah walked through the storm to Timothy's townhome to put the food away, clean up the kitchen, and feed Midnight.

And I tried to make the night a little less cold by taking the trip with him.

JANUARY 18, 2020

Be kind: Learn to be a gracious taker.

This morning, I wrote fiction

This afternoon, I stopped at a memorial dinner.

This evening, my kids did all the housework, so I didn't have to do any of it.

I was supposed to attend a screenplay festival tonight, which was showcasing the work of some of my friends.

But a series of mishaps at the house, some due to the blustery winter storm, changed those plans.

But because of the kindness of Rebekah and Daniel, my youngest son, I had the night off from further responsibilities, a bit of comfort they threw my way.

I started to insist on helping…and then changed my mind.

To be a giver, one must also be a receiver. Giving is sometimes easier than receiving.

But they really are two sides of the same coin.

JANUARY 19, 2020

Be kind: Become unselfish by chipping away at it, one opportunity at a time.

As my visions of a long weekend of writing were fast disappearing, I gave them the final hack.

My sister-in-law wanted me to interview her mother, who is turning 103 at the end of this month. But her mother only had a narrow time of the day that worked, early to mid-afternoon, right when my work deadlines are heaviest.

So instead of writing fiction this afternoon, I went to the nursing home, at my suggestion.

My sister-in-law arrived early and brought doughnuts and hot coffee "because I know how much you like your coffee."

I hadn't seen her mother in a few years, but she knew exactly who I was when I walked into her room.

We spent a lovely hour as she shared the interesting details of her life and smiled for pictures.

She was humbled that I even cared to hear her stories. My sister-in-law was thankful I took the time.

I might have made progress on the novel. But would that have been the best use of my time?

JANUARY 20, 2020

Be kind: Use talents to serve self, others.

So on this last day of my three-day weekend, I did not write fiction.

Last night, I wrote out a list of projects that really needed to get done.

The list, like most of my lists, are rather ambitious.

But since today commemorates Martin Luther King and acts of service are encouraged, I felt like I should serve, too.

Serving others seems like a no-brainer (For instance, I accompanied by son Joshua, who has multiple health issues, to the doctor today).

By using a day of service to serve me?

Yes.

By clearing the piles, I can make room for new opportunities.

It's really a kindness.

JANUARY 21, 2020

Be kind: Enjoy a tall glass of lemonade.

Today was one of the those very stressful "when life gives you lemons" days.

But I also received, mostly on social media, little pockets of support in varied places from people who had no idea today was tough.

That's what makes the support sweeter.

This isn't about making lemonade with the lemons, as if I'd resort to a "low hanging fruit" type of post.

I don't think it's possible to have a completely good day.

But I also don't think it's possible to have a completely bad day.

Mister Rogers used to exhort, "Look for the helpers."

It's easy for one to say, "Don't focus on the bad. Focus only on the good."

But it's more realistic, and perhaps kinder to oneself, to let the day be what it is.

So today, I opened myself to that support and used it to turn those lemons into something refreshing, new opportunities, perhaps?

JANUARY 22, 2020

Be kind: Be the change you want to see.

By now, perhaps some of you have thought, "Why does Denise pick up after grown children?"

Because it's sometimes the kindest act.

Today, I had an extremely busy day. My work duties are being greatly altered with little time for planning. I had a workman come to the house twice.

Rebekah also had a very busy day and brought work home with her.

But she also texted Daniel and suggested how they could break up the housework.

She made dinner.

She fed the cats.

She put away four loads of laundry and vacuumed.

She cleaned up the kitchen after dinner. Daniel scooped the cat litter.

I cleaned the two bathrooms and started the dishwasher. I had time left to walk a bit and do yoga.

That's not why I sometimes pick up after grown children.

But their actions tonight made me smile.

JANUARY 23, 2020

Be kind: Don't forget to be kind to yourself.

I felt like I was coming down with a cold (or worse), so I skipped the workout and went straight to the shower and bed.

I was fine the next day, so maybe I was just overtired.

I'm not one to make excuses for cutting myself some slack.

But sometimes, I need to do just that.

So I did.

JANUARY 24, 2020

Be kind: Be part of a chain of kindness.

As I write this, an adorable "cat" calendar, featuring black and white illustrations of cats, is within view.

Cindy, Daniel's girlfriend, bought it to me. The artist drops off dozens of copies each year to the nursing home where Cindy works.

When an opening for a story arise, I'm going to call the artist.

She may not be local to the area.

But people who adore cats are.

And those people just might need a cat calendar.

JANUARY 25, 2020

Be kind: Give something away, just because.

Today I had a book signing at The Book Market in Crest Hill because another author was not able to take January.

I sold quite a few books, including a small stack to a woman from my high school years who promoted the event on Facebook.

As the event wound down, a family that looked as if they might be struggling financially were leaving with their purchases.

Impulsively, I held up two Bertrand The Mouse books and asked her to choose one.

She did and left, smiling.

JANUARY 26, 2020

Be kind: To people and toy mice.

Now that I'm hourly, I have some semblance of weekends back, something I did not have for many years. I must confess, I'm rather protective of that time.

But a local group that exists solely for the upkeep of the Barton Grande at the Rialto Square Theatre was having its annual dinner and wanted me to attend.

I couldn't do that, but I did go down to take a few photos and videos, an opportunity to stand in the balcony and watch the old theater organ rise from the floor, something I had never done.

Because I don't have a car, Timothy went with me. He took some amazing shots and had a blast seeing parts of the theater he, too, had never seen.

Oh, and we took Bertrand. We got some great shots of him, too.

When the story appeared, the group was thrilled. I hope it helps with community awareness and appreciation for their efforts, as well as increased membership and donations.

And it only took giving up an hour of my time on Sunday.

Be kind: What may not seem like a huge sacrifice to you may be huge to the one making it. Appreciate it.

Rebekah's day off is Monday, and she is as protective of her day off as I am of mine.

But she gave back today, too, in a big way.

She made two loaves of homemade bread, to eat and for an upcoming story.

And she made s'mores dip as a suggested recipe (and photos) for my story about snacks for the Super Bowl.

All of it was delicious and wonderful.

Rebekah can be known, sometimes, for being cranky. I think her kind actions should speak louder than her very loud words.

JANUARY 28, 2020

Be kind: What if today was your last day?

I worked a very chopped up day from home today.

Over the last year and a half, I'd been ghostwriting a memoir for a Joliet woman in her nineties.

She's been in and out of the hospital recently, and, as of last night, back in. Her son called to update me, and I took the time to update him on his mother's book.

Then a friend of mine with lung cancer went into the nursing home and was feeling down. So I called her, too.

These may not seem like big acts of kindness. But when work is great and deadlines tight, any deviation adds stress to my day.

Still, I can't imagine it's as stressful as dying or being the loved one of someone who might die.

There's stress, and then there's stress.

JANUARY 29, 2020

Be kind: Pay attention to fleeting kindnesses.

Like the car that let me, on foot walking to work, let me go first.

Or the high school boy with the backpack who walked around me, in the snow, so I could keep on the sidewalk.

Or my boss who was under the gun and gave me more than five minutes today, even though I needed only five, to make sure an issue was addressed. I don't even remember the issues, but I remember the time he made.

I came home with a headache, and I rarely have headaches. Is it the weather?

But Rebekah and Daniel had split up most of the chores, except for the bathrooms. It made the rest of the night very easy.

And they didn't even know my head hurt. They did it just because.

JANUARY 30, 2020

Be kind: Ignore the technology haters.

Today I was able to touch base with one of my stepsons who had some medical tests today. I remembered to call him because of Google calendars.

Turns out he had the flu, too.

I was able to be kind and considerate, all because of technology.

Well, not all because of technology.

But also because I inconvenienced myself to enter the upcoming test in my calendar and then to inconvenience myself to reach out.

Technology is a wonderful tool to foster kindness.

Be kind: It's a gift when someone shares his or her dream. Appreciate it.

Today was a day of kindness exchanges.

Jasmine received free tickets to a full day of baking workshops in Chicago, so she invited Rebekah to participate with her. When she stopped at my house before dawn (they had a train to catch), Jasmine had coffee for me, Timothy, and Daniel, and tea for Rebekah, very sweet of her.

I worked hard and fast all day so I could help Timothy test drive cars. It's his goal to buy a new one this year, so I can have access to his old one. I opted to go carless years ago to put all my money into our living arrangement. This took the financial heat off my youngest kids. They, in turn, put their money into new, reliable cars, so they could accept any job opportunity that put them ahead.

During one test run, the conversation turned to Timothy's career as a corporate chef. Immediately our salesman lit up and he began to talk to Timothy about his dream of opening a sandwich shop featuring specialty breads. He spent more time showing us videos of breads than trying to sell Timothy a car.

It was beautiful to watch and hear, the way this man lit up talking about sandwiches.

Timothy didn't buy a car that night. But he did validate another person's dream.

FEBURARY 1, 2020

Be kind: Don't be stingy when others want to treat you.

Someone bought tickets for us to attend a sold-out chocolate ball. It wasn't my first choice for a Saturday night (I wanted to write), but the person who bought them was super-excited to treat us.

Besides, I could cover the event for The Herald-News, too, and make next week easier, so off to the ball we went.

Our benefactor, who was working the event, felt supported. The food vendors felt supported. The organization felt supported.

I had fun with my family.

Win-win-win-win.

FEBRUARY 2, 2020

Be kind: Don't take the small kindnesses of others for granted.

Every Saturday and Sunday Rebekah likes to go to the gas station near our home for unsweetened iced tea for her and a small bold coffee for me.

Every Sunday, a man who hangs out there, opens the door for us and has a Sunday Herald-News open to the features section because I like to look at my pages in print.

This has gone on for years.

Later that day, Timothy and Rebekah insisted we go shoe shopping. Timothy needed shoes; Rebekah wanted to look; and I needed shoes, too, but I hate shopping, so I tend to put it off.

Oh, and I have a hard time finding shoes that fit, too. But Rebekah is great with foot care, including my feet.

This is how we shop: I sit on a chair and she brings shoes she thinks might fit. I try them on, walk a few paces, and say "yay" or "nay." It's usually nay.

Today, I came home with two yays because others cared enough about my feet to see I'm duly shod.

FEBRUARY 3, 2020

Be kind: get out of the way.

Today is Monday, Rebekah's day off. We're a family of weird introverts. We need time and space to recharge, alone, in an empty house.

So on Sunday nights, I try to ensure the housework is done, and that I hurry out of the house as soon as I've fed the cats lunch.

It's a small consideration, but it means a lot to Rebekah.

FEBRUARY 4, 2020

Be kind: The right phone call at the right time can brighten a dreary day.

A friend of mine from high school is in a nursing home with cancer.

I talked to her briefly this morning. She told me she hasn't been bathed in days, no one is turning her, and requests for ice and hot chocolate have gone unheeded.

So I called her nurse. I was pleasant, acknowledged the fact she and her staff were busy, and, when they had time, could they help out?

They did. My friend was thrilled.

She's still dying of cancer.

But, for that day, at least, she was clean, comfortable, and refreshed.

FEBRUARY 5, 2020

Be kind: A few minutes of extending yourself can make a big difference in someone's career.

By Tuesday night, I had my stories ready for Thursday's paper. And then I noticed an event that could launch someone's career.

But it meant I'd have to squeeze the interview and the processing of photos and the writing and editing of the story into tomorrow morning, which was already full.

That made the day a little stressful. But the person was thrilled with the attention that dropped out of the sky.

I hoped it helped. Isn't that why God gives us talents?

FEBRUARY 6, 2020

Be kind: Shut up and listen.

Today was challenging because I lost actual work time to drive over an hour away for an all-hands meeting.

Then I had a meeting for WriteOn Joliet that night, where I help critique the work of other writers. So I arrived a bit stressed.

One of my gifts to others is my ability to listen. I like hearing people's stories, and I like sharing them.

But sometimes, I talk more than listen, especially when I'm stressed (see above) or excited. I'm working on improving this.

FEBRUARY 7

Be kind: When you're meant to be kind, doors will open.

Now that I'm hourly, I can't be as wanton in accepting every story that comes my way.

That morning, my daughter called me about an extremely sad situation. A young couple she knew just found out their toddler was full of cancer, including every bone in its body. The couple has two other young children and was already struggling financially.

I told her I would absolutely write a story, but it would have to wait a week. I was almost out of hours.

At the end of the day, my four o'clock appointment stood me up. So after I met all my deadlines, I called Sarah and asked her to connect me with the family.

It was the end of the day and a trying week, and I was ready to be done.

But I could, and did, extend myself for a family who's live will be changed forever.

I hope the story does well. I hope the community rallies around them.

FEBRUARY 8, 2020

Be kind: Sew kindness, reap kindness.

I had no plans for today except errands and getting my taxes done. This was wonderful as I really wanted to immerse myself in two novels I was writing.

But then Timothy stopped at the house to update my phone and add some features to make my life easier (all his idea), and when he was done, he came up to my room to give me a quick tutorial. That's when he noticed my monitor was blurry.

I hope to get detailed about the details. But it included several hours of Timothy hooking up his monitor, keyboard, and my mouse to his computer, adjusting the features, and then running out with Rebekah to several stores to find a giant monitor and better keyboard and mouse, all on sale.

Then he proceeded to tear everything apart to hook everything up.

And the monitor would not turn on.

More troubleshooting, and he realized he needed a special convertor cord. He asked me to run to the store with him.

We did, but the conversion didn't work. So he tore it all back down again and hooked up equipment to my computer again (He could rely on his laptop for now, he said), and went home for the night.

That left me with about two hours for a shower and some writing before I fell asleep.

It was not the day I thought I wanted.

But it allowed to bask in the goodness of a son.

Parents, keep this in mind when the baby keeps you up at night.

BTW, he was back at dawn with a new converter.

FEBRUARY 9, 2020

Be kind: Bless and be blessed.

Today Rebekah and Cindy tried to make chocolate cups from scratch so I could write about it for The Herald-News

Yesterday, Rebekah tried with molds, but the molds were flimsy and the chocolate cups broke. Timothy suggested molding chocolate around balloons.

Rebekah and Cindy tried for hours. The kitchen looked like a candy factory, and every chocolate bowl failed.

But they laughed a lot, and I wound up with a humorous column with photos and two videos.

Rebekah now has ideas for improving the process, which can only help further her pastry career.

FEBRUARY 10, 2020

Be kind: Sometimes, it really IS the thought that counts.

I tried to get out of the house a little earlier today so Rebekah, on her day off, didn't have me having around on her free day.

That didn't happen, but she was sweet about it.

Having her own room really helps, she said.

In this case, she appreciated the thought, and it seemed to count anyway.

FEBRUARY 11, 2020

Be kind: Take time to let others shine.

Yes, it's my job.

But today, I scheduled one interview right after the other, all highlighting new events or programs in the area that showcase some of the more nuanced concepts, opportunities, and talents.

Yes, I take on a lot.

As the author of the BryonySeries, the only way I can find readers who will enjoy the series is to promote, promote, promote.

Today people have so much information coming at them, it's hard to stand out.

Sometimes, I can help people with their promotion by writing their stories.

So I did.

FEBRUARY 12, 2020

Be kind: If you have the opportunity to be kind, do it.

Today I called a family-owned restaurant to schedule a story for an upcoming event.

Turns out the contact person had sent the wrong date. The event was in two days and the story needed to run tomorrow.

So I turned the morning upside down to take on a story that had to be interviewed, written, and on the page in a couple hours with other work to be done.

But the contact was so distressed, and the event was so important to them, that I did.

Yes, it made for a stressful day. But next year at this time, I won't even remember it unless I read this entry.

Everyone makes mistakes. An entire event should not be ruined due to lack of publicity because of a typo, not when I can help it.

FEBRUARY 13, 2020

Be kind: Notice and raise someone up.

I'm going to cheat on this one and direct you to a video from this day: bit.ly/2vrymFV.

I don't think I could say it as well twice.

FEBRUARY 14, 2020

Be kind: It's a day for love, even for the unlovable.

Each year, Rebekah makes little Valentine's Day gift bags for the immediate members in our family, a tradition that goes back to before she was born.

Then she treated me to dinner at Joliet Junior College's Thrive.

During the course of the evening, a source for a story wanted me to correct something in a story, and this person wanted it done ASAP. The fact that I was not working at the time or in close proximity of computer did not matter.

I could have turned off the phone and handled it later. But I decided to be kind to myself and not have it hanging over my head.

I took a few minutes and did it.

After that, I was present to my daughter and our dinner.

And I didn't have to address work when I came home full of wonderful food and coffee, happy and relaxed.

FEBURARY 15, 2020

Be kind: You can be kind to yourself and others at the same time.

Sue wanted to schedule a Barnes and Noble coffee date with Rebekah and me for today. This was the perfect weekend because I still had plenty of time for writing fiction.

But when Sue suggested noon, I suggested evening. Noon would break up my concentration, and I needed an unbroken block of hours.

So we agreed to meet at six. I spent the day writing fiction, Rebekah came out of her shell and came home with a new book, and Sue and I caught up on books, writing, life and more.

It was a pleasant day for all.

FEBRUARY 16, 2020

Be kind: Reach out to another, and respond when another reaches out to you.

After watching "Parasite" with Rebekah, my mind was too full to write dark fiction.

So while she went over to Timothy's to play video games, I cleaned up the house.

I spent a couple hours on the phone with my mother, who lives out of state, as I cleaned, and she was happy for the company.

Later, as I was catching up on some projects, so I could still write fiction tomorrow, Rebekah and Daniel came home from grocery shopping with pizza.

Rebekah had bought me a miniature Larry the Llama for traveling, and she asked if I wanted to watch a Korean drama we had started or just "do me."

I went with the drama. I still have all night and all day to be with me. Time with family, though, is fleeting.

FEBRUARY 17, 2020

Be kind: One small "click" for you, one giant help for another.

You know those "click here and vote for so and so" contests you see on social media?

Yeah, I never do those either.

Until tonight.

Someone I trusted posted one, to help a special needs child who adores bike riding to get a specially designed tandem bike.

Yes, I clicked.

And then I reached out for a story to encourage others to do so, too.

All this took less than three minutes of my time.

FEBRUARY 18, 2020

Be kind: A change in routine can change your perspective.

On Tuesdays I usually stay home for some serious power writing.

But I'd adjusted the stories I planned last week to account for having President's Day off yesterday.

Because of it, I only worked from home on Friday.

Except it made today feel like a Monday.

And tomorrow is already Wednesday.

Even though this is a compressed work week, which is stressful, the weekend, and rest from the efforts, is already in sight.

One small change can bring great cheer.

FEBRUARY 19, 2020

Be kind: Give praise.

This post is a little different than most, no anecdotes here.

Most people, you most likely included, are starving for praise, which explains why many people aren't liberal with praise.

I mean, it's impossible to feed another person dinner when you don't have food in your own house.

So start praising yourself today.

This is not a "power of positive thinking" post, and it's not a suggestion to become self-absorbed.

But perhaps take three times each day to praise yourself for something you did well, or for how nice you looked in that shirt, or for taking the time to help another.

You get the idea.

Now do that three times for three other people. Do that every day.

This is what will happen.

You will become less dependent on other people's approval.

And you will be sharing from an overflowing larder of good will, thus helping to fill other individuals' need for praise, too.

OK, one anecdote.

My son Timothy is very good with praising others. Whenever we are out, he randomly compliments people on their clothes, their hair, their nails, their service, etc.

It cost him nothing but a couple sentences and a smile.

In return, he receives a huge smile and thank you from another, as well as the joy of knowing he made it happen.

FEBRUARY 20, 2020

Be kind: Let go.

Tonight at WriteOn Joliet, my co-leader really wanted to tackle some flash fiction.

But he also wanted those who didn't have the opportunity to read last time (me and a couple others) to read first.

Except the other readings were long, and time was getting tight.

So I put my reading away in favor of flash fiction.

The reading will be there next time.

My co-leader's enthusiasm for his idea may not be.

But by making my desires less immediate, we both got to shine, just at different times.

Sometimes, one person must step back.

You should not always step back. That can breed resentment and self-pity.

Learn to discern when it should be about you and when it should not.

FEBRUARY 21, 2020

Be kind: Find a compromise

Today was a long day, and I never started housework until after nine o'clock.

As I was cleaning the downstairs bathroom, a source I was trying to reach on Thursday messaged me through social media upset because I hadn't returned phone calls.

I double-checked my phone. No messages.

It turns out this source had dialed the wrong number and wanted to be interviewed now, for a story that was already on the page.

I really didn't want to redo the page. And my brain was too tired for an interview this late.

And being hourly now, I had reserved the last bit of time for an interviewing tomorrow in another town.

So I made this suggestion: I could talk on the way to tomorrow's appointment (I wasn't driving) and add a few comments to the online version of the story.

The wrong number was an honest mistake. But I didn't want to unwittingly be the cause of a second one by tearing apart a page when it was already past deadline and then rushing to put the page back together.

FEBRUARY 22, 2020

Be kind: Go the extra mile.

In this case, it was an extra seven miles, one way, to New Lenox.

But it made a man who was turning one hundred, along with his three daughters, feel special.

I had a copy of his memoir and some vintage photos for his story.

But I wanted to hear in his own voice that he wanted the story. I also shot some video and took his picture, nothing fancy, all with my cell phone.

As we talked, this man, who had worked for The Herald-News a long time ago, started asking me if I knew some of the people he had known; I hadn't.

But I did mention one name, our publisher, and his face lit up, and he got very excited. He started sharing his high opinion of this man.

Immediately, I started shooting video, not for the story, but to show my publisher, who was thrilled this man had remembered him in such a positive way.

So fourteen miles and ninety minutes of my time made for a better story and lots of happiness.

FEBRUARY 23, 2020

Be kind: waste time.

I didn't do too much today, and it sure felt good.

I tackled a few items on the BryonySeries list with Rebekah, cleaned house, took a walk, watched an Asian drama.

I did all these things in a leisurely way.

The day felt long and slow, not the case if I'd been writing fiction.

I took a writing break to let the story simmer and my mind rest.

I'm not one for wasting time, as a general rule.

If you're generally a timewaster, this entry may not apply to you.

But for those of us who live very full days every day, a bit of timewasting is in order.

The rejuvenation only makes us more effective when we return to "full."

FEBRUARY 24, 2020

Be kind: Celebrate your daily accomplishments.

Timothy put a "note" app on my phone that's great for keeping track of my daily "to-do" lists.

When I wrote them by hand, I had to keep rewriting them and updating them.

With this app, I can just update as needed.

Plus, and this is a featured he added, each task has a little box next to it.

When I finish it, I add a check to the box. The entire task fades (but is still legible), and I can see the check in the box.

At the end of the day, instead of feeling stressed over what did not get done, I can see all the check marks and congratulate myself for what I did complete.

Too often, we focus on our failures.

Yes, we need to learn from them.

But we can also learn to celebrate our successes, what we did right, even if no one else notices or comments.

FEBRUARY 25, 2020

Be kind: Be open to spontaneous opportunities for kindness.

Today was National Pancake Day.

And today nine of us (including three young children) wound up at the International House of Pancakes for dinner – free short stacks along with some paid orders, an entirely last-minute decision that gave us some great time for unexpected bonding.

All this in a snowstorm. And then bowling.

Too many people talked at once when placing our orders. But the waitress was patient and upbeat and took all the confusion in stride.

One of my sons tipped her well when we left. My son and his wife had already bundled up the restless kids and were heading to the parking lot.

I and another adult child were the last to leave. The two tables looked as if forty people had eaten there. So we took a few minutes to consolidate the dishes and clean up the mess.

Yes, she gets paid to work there. But servers generally aren't making top dollar, and she's not our personal maid.

And it only took a few minutes of our time to make her night easier.

FEBRUARY 26, 2020

Be kind: Do your part.

Ever wonder how so and so can get away with breaking the rules while you cannot?

I'm not suggesting you should break rules, of course.

But you know the scenario. A certain person gets away with certain behavior all the time, and you think to yourself, "If I did that, I'd be in trouble."

It's frustrating when you're working hard to cross all the t's and dot all the i's and someone else consistently drops the ball.

The temptation to slack off is understandable. Don't give in!

If something needs to be addressed, then do it respectfully.

If it's not your place to address, keep doing your part and do it well to the best of your ability. Then your conscience will be clear, and you will feel at ease with yourself.

FEBRUARY 27, 2020

Tough day? Be kind: Cut everyone some slack.

Today everyone got home late from work.

The house didn't look too bad, but we try to keep up on daily chores, so they don't get away from us.

Tonight, we made a mutual agreement to touch up a few things and call it a night.

Everyone was stressed and tired and needed some downtime.

It's not a reason to not do housework most of the time.

But tonight, that reason was good enough.

FEBRUARY 28, 2020

Be kind: Show kindness with your presence.

Tonight I attended a friend's book signing, and tomorrow I will do the same.

I already own all the books for the first friend, so I didn't buy any. But I did take photos and a video to share on social media.

Tomorrow, I will buy two from the second friend and take more photos.

But the kindness is not just in the purchase – although, as an author, I know how appreciated the purchases are.

The kindness is in the physical presence.

It's unnerving to host a public event and wonder if people will attend. Unfortunately, most people don't like to be the first attendee to the party.

Yet, bodies will attract bodies. Meaning your very presence might encourage someone else to pop in.

But it's not just author events where simply showing up is kindness. It's taking the time to attend a wake, a vendor fair, a fundraiser, any situation where someone might need the support of a person's physical presence.

Can't attend? Send a little note, a text, a Facebook message expressing your best, and most sincere wishes. It will be nearly as appreciated.

FEBRUARY 29, 2020

Be kind: When you're wrong, don't argue.

Today I had to file a story late and set it for web publication for a certain time.

I'm not certain how I messed up the time, but it looked right when I scheduled it.

I left the house to run two errands and when I returned, I had an email saying it was scheduled at the wrong time. So I corrected it.

As soon as I did it, I had an upset phone call saying not to do it.

Well, too late.

The person on the other end was understandably upset and told me never to schedule anything ever again.

Lesson here: When someone is upset with you, no matter how unreasonable it may seem to you, it's kinder to everyone to be silent in the moment.

Yes, mistakes happen.

But when your mistake, however unintentional, becomes someone else's problem, the present time might not be the best time to defend yourself. It only makes tempers escalate. Besides, the matter may only be an issue in the moment and quite forgotten later.

If not, and an accounting must be made at some point, distance makes for a more rational and cool discussion.

Either way, no one winds up saying anything that contributes to a rift.

If you can't be right, you can still be kind.

And if you feel badly about making a mistake, and it's eating at you, the best remedy is still to not argue. Instead, take the time in that moment to do something nice for someone.

This way, everyone wins.

MARCH 1, 2020

Be kind: Let people finish talking.

I don't like to waste people's time.

Maybe that's because I've spent a few decades in journalism when minutes and seconds count.

So when people are giving me information I already know or information that's heading in the wrong direction, I've developed a bad habit of cutting them off.

That may help with brevity, but it's rude.

I think that it might be better to let people finish their thoughts and then respond.

At any rate, I'm going to try it.

MARCH 2, 2020

Be kind: Let someone else go first.

Let someone go ahead of you in line.

Just because.

People fight big and small battles all day long.

A simple "No, please; you go ahead" might be just the day brightener a harried, weary person needs.

MARCH 3, 2020

Be kind: Be the morning sun on social media.

People's newsfeeds are full of "me, me, me" and negative rants.

Let your first post of the day be something pretty, inspiring, or even a quick, "I hope all my friends are well today," to let the people to whom you are connected virtually know that you genuinely care.

MARCH 4, 2020

Be kind: Straighten up your desk before you go home.

After my dad retired and set up a home office in the basement to work on home inspections, he kept regular start and stop times, along with a noon break for lunch.

When the day ended, he put the paperwork away, placed the pencils into their holders, brushed the desk clean, shut down the computer, and clicked off the light.

I do the same at my work office. And I try to do the same at home, too.

It's a routine that will help you transition out of work into the next part of your day.

And you won't feel overwhelmed by clutter when the next day's work begins.

MARCH 5, 2020

Be kind: Read a book by a local author

And don't try to fake it by skimming the book or speed reading through it.

You might have to try a couple books before you find one that resonates with you.

If you really don't like a book, give it to a friend who might enjoy it or donate it to a thrift shop. This will give the opportunity of discovery to another reader who doesn't have the money to pay full price.

When you find that special book, send a note to the author and recommend it on your social media posts. It's a kindness that goes beyond free marketing for the writer.

It gives other readers the chance to enjoy an unknown title by an unknown author.

Avid readers are almost always delighted by that type of surprise.

MARCH 6, 2020

Be kind: Take out the garbage

Let's face it. That's a job most people don't like to do.
So for a day, a week, a month, or forever, shoulder the responsibility of one of the ickiest jobs in the house.

It's a double kindness.

You'll feel good about your generosity.

And the other people in the home will feel relieved – and maybe even loved.

MARCH 7, 2020

Be kind: Take some local art home.

The amount of time an artist spends making art is far, far more than the amount of time someone, even many someones, can appreciate.

If the artist is a local artist, that appreciation (after appreciation given by family and friends) can be negligible.

And yet, decorating an entire house in locally made art will give you a subtle sense of connectedness to your community, even if you live alone.

At the very least, consider purchasing at least one piece that you like (don't insult an artist by gushing over something that leaves you feeling meh; be genuine), displaying it, and then sending a note (email will do) to the artist a year later, letting that artist know how much you are still enjoying the piece.

MARCH 8, 2020

Be kind: Give someone your full attention.

Let someone else do the talking and listen carefully.

You will never have to fumble for conversation openers again.

And you will give a gift few people ever receive.

MARCH 9, 2020

Be kind: Ask someone you know for advice.

Most people are experts in at least one area. Most people never get to share what they know.

Make a list (mental or physical) of all the people you know. Next to their names, add their areas of expertise.

When you need advice, you can quickly go to a trusted source, all the while strengthening the bonds between you and the people you know.

MARCH 10, 2020

Be kind: don't smite the bearer of the news.

Today I learned that my insurance company will no longer pay for the drug that has kept me asthma-free since 2007.

Now I have some options: try a different drug and risk undoing the remission or pay full price for the new drug.

Since it took many years and many drugs to get me to my current healthy status, I didn't wish to undo that progress.

So I decided to keep accepting side editing work to build up a fund to pay for the medicine.

My kids sprang into action, too, by searching online for coupons to reduce the cost.

One good outcome: I no longer feel at the mercy of the insurance company about this drug. I only need to worry if the manufacturer stops making it (unlikely, but you never know).

Also, I'm very proud of myself for conducting myself like a reasonable human being as I discussed options with the representatives at my doctor's office, my pharmacy, and the manufacturer of the drug.

Because none of these people made the decision to quit paying. And being rude to them would only blight their day while not solving the problem.

I even remembered to thank them for their help, quite a feat when my mind is whirling with frustration and panic.

MARCH 11, 2020

Be kind: Remember, we're all on the same journey.

Today that journey was chaos.

The pandemic that I feared was impending when I wrote the first story about the novel coronavirus for my company, back when few took it seriously, is at the doorstep.

Today I couldn't make phone calls and write stories fast enough before the information changed. I could hear the voices of the people I interviewed trying to communicate new information to the community, even as the people communicating the information were rapidly making those adjustments.

To survive these challenges, we must lose the us-them mentality. It's "we."

And "we" must work together to defeat this virus.

Or the virus may defeat us.

And them.

MARCH 12, 2020

Be kind: Make someone laugh.

Today was a high stress day, but no one can avoid high stress days in their life.

But we can make them more pleasant.

If you are the one experiencing high stress, you can remind yourself that this will pass – because it will.

But find a moment of relief: surf the web and find a joke, or funny video clip, or meme to break the hard ice of STRESS.

And if you're having a good day, do these things for someone else.

MARCH 13, 2020

Be kind: Forgive.

Yesterday the company sent us home to work remotely. We could leave after lunch or at the end of the workday.

I couldn't go home until the end of the workday, so I remained in the office.

The reason why I couldn't go home is because a workman was there, fixing a problem caused by another tenant in the same building.

The issue caused us some grief.

But the tenant in question is long gone. So of what value is nursing anger or holding a grudge?

None.

So I let it go.

MARCH 14, 2020

Be kind: Keep up with technology.

Yesterday I logged into my first Zoom meeting.

It was supposed to be an in-person, all-hands company meeting, but we were sent home yesterday to work from home until April.

So the meeting was virtual, and I did just fine with the process.

I may be slower than young people in adjusting because I didn't grow up with the technology and never played video games, even as an adult.

But that doesn't mean I can't move forward, too.

MARCH 15, 2020

Be kind: Eat and drink slowly.

Savor each bite and sip.

You'll be satisfied sooner and less inclined to overindulge.

Your waistline, blood pressure, pancreas, and self-esteem will thank you.

MARCH 16, 2020

Be kind: Be patient when others are learning your skills.

Today was my first day of officially working full-time from home.

I'm a former freelance writer, so I'm not only used to working at home, I love working from home and often worked from home even before today.

However, not everyone finds this easy. So be patient when others are struggling with skills that come easy to you.

I honestly think this will not end in April.

MARCH 17, 2020

Be kind: Absorb the essence of holidays.

Today is the feast day of St. Patrick. For some, it's a day for wearing green, eating corned beef, and drinking lots of beer.

But is that the heart of the day, especially for a sober-minded saint?

Even after you strip away the myths, the remaining factual details should inspire anyone: sharing truth and speaking out for justice and equality.

Besides, you can always wear green, eat corned beef, and drink beer on Calkins Day.

MARCH 18, 2020

Be kind: Remember from whence you came.

A lot of people are losing their jobs right now. But the plight might be especially perilous for one group of people who don't typically qualify for unemployment benefits.

Freelancers.

When I was a freelance writer, people used to assume that, because I worked for myself, I could take off work anytime I wished.

But that wasn't true. If I didn't work, I didn't get paid. I worked every day, every holiday. I had contracted the work, and the work needed to be done.

Now I didn't necessarily work all day, every day. But I rarely skipped an entire day.

So I wrote a story for The Herald-News about the anxiety several local freelancers were feeling to bring, if anything, awareness to their situation.

We tend to forget from whence we came once we're past it. But that's not wise.

If you've been poor, don't forget the poor.

If you've gone hungry, don't forget the hungry.

If you've lost weight, encourage those who are struggling.

You get the idea.

MARCH 19, 2020

Be kind: Keep the trust.

Today I wrote a story about a person who shared what it's like to be tested for the coronavirus.

No one locally, to my knowledge, has publicly shared the details of the process.

This person asked to remain anonymous, due to concerns about losing employment.

If you're asked to keep a confidence, be sure to keep it, unless keeping it leads to harm for you or another.

Think of the high regard a person has for you to share something that's hard to share.

Don't squander it.

MARCH 20, 2020

Be kind: Let people talk just to talk.

So much of the time, we listen for two reasons.

One is to get information.

The other is waiting our turn to talk.

Sometimes, people just need to talk, not because they want you to solve their problems but just to talk.

So listen and let them talk.

MARCH 21, 2020

Be kind: Stay at home.

This is an easy way to be kind to yourself and others.

You limit the chances of getting sick, and you limit the chances for others.

MARCH 22, 2020

Be kind: Walk and talk.

Feet in motion, and ears in gear is the way to stay healthy and connected.

If walking around your neighborhood is boring, make a phone call while you walk.

Your mind, body, and loved ones will thank you.

MARCH 23, 2020

Be kind: Banish useless worry.

Scared of catching the coronavirus?

Be prudent, follow mitigations, and don't give anxiety a foothold, even if you need professional help to get there.

By fretting over something that hasn't happened, you ruin the serenity of the now.

MARCH 24, 2020

Be kind: Don't waste this time.

Use this time to find creative ways to communicate and catch up on the projects you've shelved until you have time.
    Now you have it.

MARCH 25, 2020

Be kind: Read.

Read a print book, read on your phone, but read.
   Reading is the doorway to knowledge and adventure.
   It's cheap; it's accessible.
   Studies show it fosters empathy, improves memory, and may reduce the risk for developing Alzheimer's later in life.
   If you're not a reader, now's a good time to start.
   If you are a reader, keep up the good work.

MARCH 26, 2020

Be kind: Make new routines.

Missing old routines by staying home? Make new ones.

For instance, my son Timothy and I have been taking two-hour walks after dinner each night.

We're exploring different neighborhoods on foot, catching up on each other's work projects, sharing news on the coronavirus and our economic and health concerns, talking technology, and sharing ideas for future books in The Adventures of Cornell Dyer series we're writing.

If our normal routine weren't altered, we wouldn't have this one. So that's one blessing that's come out of this crazy state of the world right now.

Even this routine will pass. And then you know what?

You'll be kind to yourself and make another new one.

MARCH 27, 2020

Be kind: Call to mind challenges overcome

This date in 1982 was my due date for my first child.

I didn't feel well and slept a lot. My husband was being laid off from Caterpillar in Joliet, one week every month.

I couldn't wait to go back to my comfortable old life.

I was too immature and inexperienced to realize my old life had passed away for a better one.

Looking back, I'm glad for the new life.

Maybe one day years from now, we'll feel the same about the things 2020 stripped from us.

MARCH 28, 2020

Be kind: Give a hug to someone in your household who needs it

And if you're living alone and staying at home, hug yourself, too.

Sounds stupid? Not at all. Before you can love and affirm other, you must love and affirm yourself.

MARCH 29, 2020

Be kind: Be creative in bridging the social gap.

Here's what some local teachers did: bit.ly/3dFz1F4.
Cool, right?

Be kind: Share three talents of loved ones with others.

Today is the birthday of my oldest son, Christopher David.

If you have any computer hardware problems, he is the person to call. He is a self-taught computer expert, and he is savvier and more knowledgeable and better at troubleshooting than information technology experts at many companies. He built my computer from spare parts a few years ago, and it works better than any computer I've ever owed.

Except for the first laptop (a Christmas gift), I've only used refurbished laptops from Christopher. He simply swaps them out from time to time and moves all files to the new one while I drink a cup of coffee.

He values family and family traditions.

He will extend himself to help another, especially if that person has an immediate car problem.

MARCH 31, 2020

Be kind: Be present to another's sufferings.

Today I interviewed the first local person willing to discuss his experiences with COVID-19.

He talked a very long time. I could feel the fear, the anxiety, the thankfulness to be alive.

I tried to reproduce all of that in the story, along with the information readers want: knowledge of the experience of this terrible virus.

Mostly, he wanted to share his story.

So I listened carefully so I could do just that.

APRIL 1, 2020

Be kind: Shrug it off.

Today someone who scheduled an interview with me changed her mind. And I get it.

That person works in health care. And that person was going to share what it's like working in health care with this very scary virus.

But now that person feels the supervisor won't like it.
I understand.

Yes. I understand.

I would have loved writing this story, especially since I blocked a good deal of time to let this person talk. But I understand.

That was a deliberate act of kindness on my part.

I did more than simply accept and shrug it off.

I understood.

APRIL 2, 2020

Be kind: Find a solution to a need.

Tonight, WriteOn Joliet goes virtual for the first time with a Zoom meeting. It's not ideal. But it's better than no meeting.

We skipped last month before of the stay at home order. The order is now extended, at least in Illinois.

I feel the writers may need the group more than ever now. Writing requires isolation to write. But eventually writers need readers and feedback.

The virus is working very hard to keep people apart.

But when humans have hope, we don't let evil have the last word, even if it talks very loudly for a while.

Be that hope for someone.

Be the person who finds a way.

APRIL 3, 2020

Be kind: Have one night of magic each week.

I'm such a kid when it comes to Friday nights. Yippee! I don't have to go to work tomorrow. I can stay up late, drink coffee, and write fiction!

Friday nights, for me, feels like summer vacation. A weekend of possibilities stretches forth forever.

It's untrue, of course. But the feeling is delicious. Friday night is the most magical night of the week for me.

What makes you feel that way? A bath and candles? Carryout when you cook all the time? Or trying a new recipe when you've eaten lots of carryout? A walk in the park or a drive down an unfamiliar road? Writing? Painting? Praying?

Whatever takes you to "nirvana," be kind to yourself and indulge yourself at least once each week.

APRIL 4, 2020

Be kind: Take an afternoon nap.

Even if you don't actually go to sleep, take twenty, thirty, sixty minutes, and be lazy.

Snuggle under that afghan over the couch or on your bed and drift off.

Because you can.

Life is full and busy for most of us. To allow yourself the luxury of just relaxing is heavenly and refreshing.

APRIL 5, 2020

Be kind: Be open to dialogue.

I'm currently working on a first draft of a new novel. Another local writer reached out and offered to read some of those drafts and give feedback.

So I sent what I'd written so far.

It came back with criticism before the writer had read one chapter. The writer didn't like the premise or the outline and thought I should write a different novel from a different perspective. The chapters were, needless to say, pretty marked up.

But the writer offered a phone conversation, too. Of course I agreed. It gave this person the opportunity to discuss why the novel was a bad idea. It gave me a chance to discuss why I wanted to write this novel.

Yes, I'm going ahead and writing it.

But I also saved those marked up chapters. They will be useful during the revision process.

Just because we didn't agree on some aspects doesn't mean the markups don't have value.

Praise tastes good, and everyone needs a little ice cream from time to time.

Broccoli doesn't taste as good, but it's better for me.

Listening to another point of view gives you an opportunity to see your ideas from different perspectives.

A wider view is more apt to benefit you than a narrow one.

APRIL 6, 2020

Be kind: Give the gift of forgiveness.

If a person asks your forgiveness, give it.

If a person doesn't ask for it, give it anyway.

If a person doesn't even know he/she upset you, still forgive.

I've never met a person who was harmed by forgiveness, either in the giving or the receiving.

APRIL 7, 2020

Be kind: Make lemonade from lemons.

I interviewed a local business today that makes a product no one can use right now due to COVID-19.

So he's using his materials to make face shields for essential workers.

What can't you do because of the coronavirus?

What can you do better because of it?

APRIL 8, 2020

Be kind: Show particular love.

Years ago when my oldest son Christopher was eight years old, he bought me a Christmas present that he felt I wanted more than anything else in the entire world. He was fairly quivering with excitement when I opened it.

It was a deck of addition flashcards.

You see, I was home-schooling him and his two younger siblings at the time. The youngest and I needed the flashcards, to help him master this important math concept. But the cards had mysteriously disappeared, and every place seemed to sell cards for every operation except addition.

Somehow, my son had found a deck. And he bought them for me, with his own money he had earned from doing chores around the house.

Fast forward about thirty years. The same son has disabilities and is a self-taught computer genius.

On Christmas Day a few years ago, he showed up to my house with a built-from-parts computer. The inside glowed in my two favorite colors (blue and purple). He felt my computer was out-of-date and needed replacing. I'm still using this Christmas computer, and it's the best computer I've ever owned.

Both times he saw the need and met it, a kindness I appreciate every day.

APRIL 9, 2020

Be kind: Give a specific compliment.

Don't just say, "Good job!"

And don't just say, "You look nice today."

Say instead, "I was really impressed with that story you wrote. The main character reminded me of my best friend next door, and I felt her sadness when her grandmother died."

Say instead, "That blouse really brings out the color of your eyes. You should wear blue more often."

Vague praise, however well-intended, often sounds like empty flattery.

A specific, well-deserved, on-target compliment shows you care enough to notice and mention it.

APRIL 10, 2020

Be kind: Make something right.

I don't like problems. So I like fixing them – to make them go away.

This attitude got me in trouble quite a few times in the first and second grades. The nuns would say, "If you make a mistake, leave it."

But if I accidentally colored "red" in the "brown" spot, I would color over it to fix it.

I still feel the same way today. If I make a mistake, I hurry to find out what's incorrect and then hurry to make it right.

I try to apply that to my relationships, my job, my health.

I don't always get it right. But I try to repair it when I get it wrong.

APRIL 11, 2020

Be kind: Bury the past.

Let yesterday stay in yesterday.

Otherwise yesterday's mistakes will haunt your todays.

And yesterday's laurels will prevent you from moving forward.

Honor yesterday by cherishing the positive and learning from the negative.

But let today be today.

APRIL 12, 2020

Be kind: Be an Easter audience.

Our family is Eastern Orthodox, so we will celebrate Easter next week.

But whether one celebrates this Sunday or next Sunday, the celebrations will be similar – not in church, due to the coronavirus.

One pastor in assisted living decided to sit outside his balcony with his guitar and sing. He refused to let a nasty virus kill the message of the resurrection.

So one of my sons and I went out.

He drove and listened.

I recorded it for The Herald-News.

All three of us, plus anyone who heard it, were blessed by his kindness.

APRIL 13, 2020

Be kind: When loss is great, be extra sensitive.

Today I wrote a tribute about a special needs young woman who died of COVID-19.

She was a beautiful, happy woman. I felt honored to listen to her mother share the woman's story so readers can be inspired.

Listening with two ears is always the kind thing to do.

But be especially gentle and attentive when loss is tragic.

APRIL 14, 2020

Be kind: Be someone worth watching.

Because whether you like it or not, someone is almost always watching.
What are they seeing?

APRIL 15, 2020

Be kind: Don't say, "Take care." Reach out and actually care.

When we were still living in Channahon but with eventual foreclosure in sight, our water heater burst on Dec. 13, 2011.

It was the second time for that model, so the warranty was no good. We were struggling to buy food much less a water heater.

I remember Rebekah boiling water for washing people and dishes, while saying, "I feel so 'Little House,'" a reference to books by Laura Ingalls Wilder.

I posted something silly on social media: "I wish I was in hot water."

A Facebook friend, someone I'd never met in person, messaged me, asking how she could help. I explained our dilemma, tight budget, and everybody's crazy work schedules.

She offered to start calling around to stores to find the best price, even haggling if necessary.

She also contacted a relative of hers who worked in HVAC and asked him to install it, for free, after work. Then she ordered pizza for us, to spare us having to figure out dinner, too.

We simply had to pick up the water heater and pay for it.

The man worked late that night and didn't make it to our house until very late. But he stayed until the water heater was installed, about 10 p.m.

He was visibly tired and happy to help.

Sometimes the most we can say is "Take care."

But sometimes we can do a little more.

I still tell this story, and I'm still thankful for the kindness of a Facebook friend I've still not met in person.

APRIL 16, 2020

Be kind: Share three talents of loved ones with others.

Today is my sister's birthday. Her name is Karen Ann.

She loves reading and books so much she worked for booksellers and then worked very hard to earn her master's degree in library science. She shares her love of reading and books as a teen librarian.

She loves reading and books so much that she's rescued many books over the years from the trash and brought them to my children to read.

She loves reading and books so much that she's introduced my kids to stories and authors they might never have read.

My sister has singlehandedly done more for the cause of literacy and reading for the joy of reading than any three people I know.

APRIL 17, 2020

Be kind: Be flexible

We had a workman in my townhome today, so Timothy not only let me work at his home, he let me work at his computer and set everything up for my comfort.

Later that night, I interviewed a nurse form Edward Hospital who works in the COVID-19 unit. She works long days, so she could not talk until then.

I met all my deadlines despite the topsy turvy nature of the day because Timothy was kind enough to be flexible.

Surely, I could do the same for a nurse who's busy saving lives all day.

APRIL 18, 2020

Be kind: Be sensitive to another's loss, especially when you don't understand it.

I did not grow up in a family that made traditions.

But I did start developing traditions in childhood. Some of those traditions included making gifts, listening to festive Christmas records, and tapping into certain moods when decorating Christmas trees and wrapping gifts.

I felt families should have traditions. So I began forming those traditions when I began forming a family.

The COVID-19 pandemic has blown a hole into the cherished traditions of many this year, traditions that usually revolve around togetherness.

Many people have felt that loss acutely and painfully than others whereas others have adapted more quickly, more easily.

Wherever you are on that grief/adaptation scale, tread lightly and be aware of that loss in others, for its all too easy to be dismissive if we're handling it OK or unaware of another's pain when we're awash in our own.

Be kind: Make something.

For us as Eastern Orthodox Christians, Holy Week is the most solemn time of the year – with Easter being the most joyful.

All of Lent is a journey of fasting in various forms and a process of self-emptying in order to receive something greater and better.

Lent in the Eastern Orthodox church has the same themes each year at the same time. And that journey takes us to the Cross and then to the Tomb and then to the Empty Tomb, where we rejoice with the feasting of traditional foods and gladness.

Our church has services to go with this journey. And we missed every one of them this year because our particular church home is not doing virtual services.

We could have tapped into another church's virtual services. For reasons of our own, we passed.

We did prepare the traditional foods, and four of us (we all live together) partook of them together.

In the moment, they felt a little hollow all by themselves.

But I think when we look back at this time, we will see that we lived the Lenten journey in 2020. The actual "new life" is still in the future.

However, we could still live in that faith and promise – and hold fast to "behold I make all things new."

So we made something new.

The day was sunny and mild, so Timothy and Daniel removed the winter grime from their cars through washing and waxing.

And Rebekah and I made paper Victorian Easter hats. It was our first attempt at paper crafts, and they did not turn out too shabby, I think.

I posted pictures on my blog. To see them, visit bit.ly/2WPnOdK.

APRIL 20, 2020

Be kind: Get dressed.

While we were working tonight, Timothy showed me an article on his phone about how people aren't getting dressed or even bathing regularly during this pandemic.

Because they have nowhere to go, people don't see the point of a daily shower, washing their face and brushing their teeth in the morning, or putting on clean clothes.

He was surprised. And so was I. I think the only time I've skipped some of those basics was the first night after surgery.

Such an article is really "telling" on the state of our view of ourselves.

If the only reason we brush our teeth is for someone else's opinion, we need a reality check.

I recently read a lovely blog. The writer had shared her mother's daily makeup routine, which had spanned decades.

I don't remember all of the details, and I appear not to have bookmarked it. I believe the mother had been a single, working mom and most likely had a million reasons to skip her routine "this one time."

I do remember this Mom won a magazine contest with her morning makeover. It was that carefully and professionally done.

But this was the part that struck me. The writer said her mother viewed it as more than routine and self-care. It was a type of meditation.

Each morning this woman faced herself in the mirror and quietly watched herself take the time to care for herself before heading off to meet the challenges of the day.

APRIL 21, 2020

Be kind: Inspire others to connect.

A new trend is popping up in the pandemic: social distance parades.

People are organizing drive-byes past their loved ones' homes on their special days.

Because people can't gather in person, they still want to show they care and to join in the celebration.

I'm in awe of the resiliency of the human spirit and the way one act of good will can foster more and more of them.

APRIL 22, 2020

Be kind: Rejoice in a competitor's triumph.

That's hard to do, isn't it?
Do it anyway.

APRIL 23, 2020

Be kind: Be in awe of someone's generosity.

I recently interviewed the coordinator of a church food program.

This particular church had pitched the story to me before the pandemic and, well, I've been busy with pandemic stories, to say the least.

But I finally had the opportunity to talk to the person in charge. That person isn't old enough to drink alcohol. But she is passionate about food safety, sustainability, and serving the homeless.

And COVID-19 doesn't stop her from feeding the homeless.

APRIL 24, 2020

Be kind: Appreciate another's talents.

Is it because I didn't grow up with technology? Or is it my own intellectual deficiencies that impair me?

Whatever the reason, I'm slow to learn new technology even if I'm reading through the steps. I also process certain types of information slowly.

For instance, I'm terrible at driving to an unfamiliar place if I have to watch the signs or listen a GPS give me directions.

Now I'm terrific with directions if I'm the passenger. And I'm a good driver if I'm only driving. But the two, for me, are unequally yoked.

Rebekah, on the other hand, navigates technology super easily and can quickly learn, on her own, new approaches.

When she was home-schooled and I freelanced, my office and her bedroom were next to each other. A quick, "Hey, Rebekah, how do I do this?" was often a lifesaver.

Now that both of us are temporarily working remotely, I'm extra appreciative of her skills.

The more new technology I learn, the easier some of it becomes.

But I'll never be as good as Rebekah in that regard.

And I've been trying to make it a point to tell her so.

APRIL 25, 2020

Be kind: Celebrate another's triumphs.

Speaking of Rebekah, she's made it a consistent point this year to make healthy changes.

Now she doesn't have any specific health issues, per se.

But with a history of diabetes on both sides of her parentage, she's been working hard at eating healthier the last few years.

Even with that, she's continued to gain weight. So although she has anxiety with going to the doctor (many of us do in my family, including me) she's made an appointment with my endocrinologist for June, just in case.

In addition, Rebekah's been walking each morning and night.

And she's made consistent changes to her diet.

She's discouraged with her slow progress. But I can see hints of it: clothes loosening up, some slimming in her face.

Mostly, I'm super proud of the changes she's making. Changes are hard to make, especially for someone who thrives on routine and sameness.

Rebekah is months into the changes now, and that's where many people falter. She has not.

I'm very proud of her. And I make it a point to tell her so, too.

APRIL 26, 2020

Be kind: Tell someone how nice they look – and be specific.

I know I've written this one. But I wanted to stress it again.

So many people walk around with low self-esteem. Too many people compare themselves to others and miss their own unique beauty.

Please remind them of their attractiveness.

APRIL 27, 2020

Be kind: Encourage the fainthearted.

You can do it!

Sometimes, these four words, sincerely spoken, is just what another person needs to hear.

Look in the mirror and speak them to yourself, too.

APRIL 28, 2020

Be kind: Let people (and animals) be themselves – and love them for it.

All living things have quirks or traits that make them unique. Give them the freedom to express it.

For instance, I joke that my calico Faith has Asperger's. She lives by routine and becomes anxious at disruptions to that routine.

She's the cat that always jumped onto my desk chair and nudged my hand if feeding time was a couple minutes late. ("Why, yes, Faith, it is four o'clock.").

She wants to be petted in the exact same way at the exact same time of the day (my bedtime, unfortunately).

She paces anxiously in my room if I hit snooze one too many times because, well, I should have been on my feet by now.

This is Faith. We've accepted it.

Some people don't want anyone to talk to them until they've had their first cup of coffee. Others don't want to talk about their day until they've had time to relax. Some people don't like carrots or rainy days or the feel of pleats.

Chloe, my house plant, the only plant that's not died under my watch, even prefers to be turned a certain way to the sun (although for even growth, I do rotate her).

Too often, we think our viewpoint is the only correct viewpoint. But it isn't. And everyone relaxes a little when given the freedom to be themselves.

This is why you should think just like me about this topic.

APRIL 29, 2020

Be kind: Be patient with shortcomings, especially when trying to improve.

I have shortcomings. Most people I know have one or two, as well.

I like when people understand mine and don't expect me to be as skilled as they are in their areas of expertise. Don't you?

That understanding is hard to bestow, sometimes. What is common sense to us might be a real struggle to another.

And yet, to give leeway and understanding, is such a beautiful gift, is it not?

APRIL 30, 2020

Be kind: Collaborate.

Recently I've collaborated with other writers in the parent company if The Herald-News to write one strong story that can be posted on all platforms.

It's my first experience doing so, journalism-wise.

Not every project requires collaboration. But working together halves the task and increases the productivity.

You wash the dishes and I'll dry? We do less work while enjoying each other's company.

I'll take out the garbage; you fold towels. And then soon the chores are done, and we can all relax.

MAY 1, 2020

Be kind: Remember the hungry.

The coronavirus has raised unemployment and swelled the lines at food banks.

Here's an easy way to help that won't break your personal bank.

Whenever you shop for food, pick up a few extra items. Keep it small, so you don't notice the dip in your budget: three cans of food, half a dozen boxes of macaroni and cheese.

Take them to a food depository before you even go home. If that's not feasible, take them to a neighbor you know could use them.

MAY 2, 2020

Be kind: Remember and honor the milestones of others.

Why stop at birthdays and graduations?

Remember half birthdays, name days, feast days, etc.

Be the person who remembers important days in the lives of people you love.

MAY 3, 2020

Be kind: Do your work faithfully.

The world notices the promotions, the lauds, the raises.

God notices a good job done steadily and consistently, day in and day out.

You may not get applauded for your work. You may never get a promotion. You may never see your paycheck swell with more money.

But you will feel peace in your soul at the end of every day, knowing you did your best.

MAY 4, 2020

Be kind: Share three talents of loved ones with others.

Today is the birthday of my second child, Sarah Catherine.

She is one of the most determined people you will ever meet. If she believes in getting something done, she will stop at nothing until she figures out how to do it.

She decided to get healthy a few years ago and lost an incredible amount of weight – and kept it off. She makes healthy eating and exercise a priority.

She is an extremely detailed, dedicated hard worker.

She has an eye for bargain shopping, especially clothes, like no other. I rarely buy clothes (and almost never new) unless I am visiting her in Raleigh.

Sarah picks out all the clothes, piles them into a large shopping basket, and then the three of us (Sarah, Rebekah, and me) commandeer a dressing room to try everything on.

We keep nothing unless it fits perfectly, and we like it. Most of the items cost $2 or $3. And we have more Goodwill stores to visit.

Didn't I mention that? Yes, we only shop at Goodwill.

MAY 5, 2020

Be kind: Remember those who serve.

Many people work in professions that serve others.

Many of your comforts in life are the result of another's service to you.

Take a moment and think of all the people who served you in some form today.

Thank them.

MAY 6, 2020

Be kind: Make time for those who support you.

Recently I scheduled time to talk on the phone to my very first BryonySeries fan.

For the record, she is a real fan. Meaning, she is not a member of my family or one of my friends. She lives out of state, and I have never met her in person, although she really hopes that happens someday.

In fact, we've spoken on the phone only once, back in 2013, I believe.

She now lives a bit closer to me (Kentucky instead of Utah), so if this coronavirus would ever go away, I'd love to drive down over a weekend.

We mostly talked about life things but before we hung up, she told me about a dream she had, that *Bryony* was made into a movie.

She clearly saw John Simons playing the piano. It was so clear, so vivid to her, she said.

It's not likely any of my books will become films. And even if they did, it's also unlikely that a filmmaker will create a movie that will satisfy her as much as the dream did.

That is the power of the written word.

Funny how life works out.

I scheduled a phone conversation to be kind to someone who supports me. But when I hung up, I felt even greater support.

I hope she felt the same from me.

MAY 7, 2020

Be kind: Help others help others.

Today I wrote a story about a Plainfield restaurant that's hosting a fundraiser where the proceeds will benefit its employees, all of whom are hurting financially due to furlough or reduced hours.

I can't attend the fundraiser.

But instead of beating myself up about that, I can pass along the information and opportunity to those who can.

MAY 8, 2020

Be kind: Eat one small square of chocolate a day.

Or a small piece of candy you enjoy. Here's why.

A few years ago, my blood work showed I'm slightly pre-diabetic. So I modified my already healthy diet to one that is diabetic friendly.

If I ever cross the line from "pre" to "actual," I'll have the habits in place. But shouldn't that mean I should give up the chocolate?

No.

One small piece of candy or chocolate that you enjoy keeps you from feeling deprived. I make sure I have one each day.

If that sends my blood sugar skyrocketing, I have more problems than one piece of candy. And I will have to address them.

But I won't be drowning my sorrows in a gallon of ice cream, especially since I only eat ice cream a couple times a year.

I have not eaten an entire candy bar since I was fifteen. I don't need to eat it.

I treat myself to one small piece, two at the maximum when I really splurge, of candy every day.

MAY 9, 2020

Be kind: Share a virtual cup of coffee.

A friend of mine is missing our bookstore coffee dates where we talk about books we're reading and books we're writing.

So we held a virtual coffee date.

Was it the same? No?

But it was connection. It was positive.

And in a COVID-19 world of mitigations, we can't have enough positive connections.

MAY 10, 2020

Be kind: Spend time with an older person virtually.

Like many seniors, my mother isn't very good at online searches, and she shuns social media. She's also very disconnected from her extended family.

Today when I called her for Mother's Day, I did researched names of family members online, found photos and websites, and then texted those over to her.

Just so she could see.

Just so she could know what the rest of her family is doing.

MAY 11, 2020

Be kind: Stop to pet the cat

My calico Faith wants to be petted at all the wrong times. My cat Midnight loves to be petted all the time.

I'm very busy working from home. And because that's how these things work out, when I have some downtime, the cats are napping, or busy doing cat things, or simply have no interest in being petted.

Sometimes, I stop what I'm doing to give the cat a good petting. And then, because I'm allergic to cats, I change my shirt and wash my hands and face well.

I can't always take that ten minutes for kitty love.

But I can probably do it more often than I actually do it.

Like many people, when I'm in a groove, I don't want to break that groove, especially for a cat. So my excuse is often less about deadlines and more that I don't want to be inconvenienced.

But cats, like kids, won't be here forever. And then my pristine prose won't be interrupted by a cat needing an ear scratch and some head bumps.

Stop and smell the roses. And stop to pet the cat.

MAY 12, 2020

Be kind: Text.

It's chic these days to scorn virtual modes of communication.

But a quick text or social media message can be a real day brightener.

Sometimes we hesitate because we don't have time to talk. Or we "ghost" people for the same reason.

But we can still text, "I don't have time to talk. But I thought about you today, and that made me smile. Hope you're having a great day!"

And now you've sent something people can re-read all day.

MAY 13, 2020

Be kind: Sing.

I don't know many people who adore the sound of their singing voices. I'm sure they exist. I just don't know them.

But singing at the top of your voice relaxes the muscles, floods your brain with endorphins, and makes you feel good from top to bottom.

Watch a child sing. Note the unabashed spontaneity.

If you're super self-conscious, and your singing voice is super painful to another's ears, wait until you're home alone, if that's your inclination.

But sing.

Sing in the shower (I don't, but you might like it).

Sing while washing dishes or dusting the house.

Sing just because.

But do sing.

Singing is like smiling and laughing.

You can't frown while singing.

MAY 14, 2020

Be kind: Give hope for those who grieve

It's never easy to lose a person you cherish.

It's even harder to face that loss without the support of others.

And yet, this COVID-19 pandemic has brought us virtual and drive-thru funerals.

The pandemic is forcing us to think outside of current methods and traditions.

Do you know someone who's suffering a loss? Today, right now, take that moment to reach out: a quick phone call, a text, a gif on social media.

Do it now.

MAY 15, 2020

Be kind: Keep the promises you made in love and hope

Many of us, in the exhilaration of new beginnings, make wild promises of forever.

We promise to love and cherish a significant other.

We promise to walk 10,000 steps a day.

We promise to write 10,000 words a month.

We promise never to go to bed with dirty dishes in the sink.

We promise never to raise a voice (or a hand) to the baby in our arms.

Maybe we can't keep the letter of the law.

But we ought to keep its spirit.

The pandemic has given us time to revisit and reexamine those promises.

And we should.

MAY 16, 2020

Be kind: Burn incense.

I discovered the joys of burning incense when I was fifteen after making a spontaneous decision to buy some from Spencer's Gifts in the former Jefferson Square Mall in Joliet.

My favorite scents at the time were rose, wild strawberry, African violet, musk, sandalwood, and patchouli.

Over the years, I stopped burning incense, mostly for safety reasons. I lived in small spaces and had either too many small children or too many small cats.

But "St. Nicholas" brought me some incense this past year. I burn it only my room when I'm writing fiction and at a safe distance from any cats, who are now too old to be curious about it anyway, and a safe distance from my lungs, since I has asthma.

In addition to a lovely patchouli that I bought from a street vendor last fall, I have black cherry, frankincense, and sage and citrus, scents I could not buy when I was fifteen.

If you don't like incense, the point is not the incense, of course.

The point is to remember to surround yourself with those mundane things that brighten your day.

MAY 17, 2020

Be kind: Use social media.

I know, I know. I've heard all the arguments against social media. But try this.

Pick five people a day, go to their pages, and leave a nice comment on something they've posted.

Do it the next day.

And the next day.

That's making good use of social media.

MAY 18, 2020

Be kind: Say no.

It's not negative.

Actually, it's rude for people to cross your boundaries.

I have some people in my life who want me to meet them in person.

But I'm high risk and the answer, for now, is no.

I can acknowledge that person's feelings and how he/she wants to see me.

But I have to look out for myself, too.

Especially when it's clear that the other person isn't.

MAY 19, 2020

Be kind: Share tiny flowers.

Take a picture of a pretty flower every day and make that your social media profile photo for twenty-four hours.

    You will become more attuned to the beauty in your life.

    And you will bless another's day with simple beauty, too.

MAY 20, 2020

Be kind: Carve a wellness lifestyle.

Forget about "going on a diet."

Instead, figure out what healthy foods you can eat, and how much exercise you can tolerate, and then make that part of your daily life.

And remember to include a square of chocolate after dinner.

MAY 21, 2020

Be kind: Stop

Just pause a minute.

Stop.

Look around your room, notice the sounds, the sights, the way sun comes into the room.

That's all.

We get so busy sometimes, we forget to just notice.

But even a mini break can be rejuvenating.

MAY 22, 2020

Be kind: Wear a facemask.

I know this is controversial
    But even if you don't believe it helps, even if you argue that even the health experts go back and for on it, ask yourself this?
    Does it hurt to wear one?
    And what if it DOES help?

MAY 23, 2020

Be kind: Sleep on fresh sheets.

I have an interesting Saturday routine: I strip my bed to the mattress and wash all the sheets and blankets.

It's a bit of a pain as I find stripping and making beds tedious, and I have lots of pillows and blankets.

But it does feel wonderfully fresh when I climb into bed at night, a marvelous way to start a new week. Honestly, if I had the time, I'd choose fresh sheets every day.

I'm glad I adopted this habit. Because I had to throw my very old mattress away right before the world shut down.

Fortunately, Timothy had an air mattress to lend me. By Saturday, it needs more air. So before the sheets go on, the mattress must go up.

MAY 24, 2020

Be kind: Clear a small patch of clutter.

We often don't do a little until we can do a lot.

But we can always do a little. That stack of stuff on the kitchen table. Clear it now.

See how nice that looks?

MAY 25, 2020

Be kind: Remember those who fought for your freedom.

Take a moment of silence on Memorial Day to reflect on those who lost their lives so you could live in freedom.

Memorial Day is not just a day for cookouts.

MAY 26, 2020

Be kind: Do it now.

The associate pastor at our church gave a sermon a few years ago about his tendency to put stuff off.

So he devised a mantra for himself, which he shared with us: Do it now.

Our pastor later shared that if he doesn't do a particular task when it comes to mind, he never remembers "later."

Obviously, I can't stop in the middle of a deadline to attend to that random item in my brain.

But I can take a moment to jot it down on the list at my left (always keep a list at your left).

I review that list from time to time during the day. Most of the time, I've forgotten what I've jotted and think, "Oh, yeah. I've got to do that."

So do it now.

Or, at the very least, make a note of it now. Your future self will be so glad.

MAY 27, 2020

Be kind: Listen to a new song.

Pick something random.

A new tune brings a new perspective.

Or ask a friend to share a song he or she likes.

You'll hear new music and gain new insight into the music that moves your friend.

MAY 28, 2020

Be kind: Pause for rainbows.

While walking with Timothy tonight, we saw a majestic rainbow, so we paused to admire it and photograph it.

Notice the rainbows in your life. They may be fleeting, But they are there.

MAY 29, 2020

Be kind: Straighten your desk before you stop work for the day.

The morning will not feel so overwhelming.
    Try it and see.

MAY 30, 2020

Be kind: Empower a child.

Today I interviewed an eight-year-old Christian rapper with a faith-filled message.

He's obviously spent time around adults who care about his talent and his soul.

The next generation will be blessed because of it.

MAY 31, 2020, 2020

Be kind: Strive to do the right thing, always.

On Sunday evening, after a long day at the keyboard, I grabbed Rebekah for a walk.

I heard loud noises that sounded like fireworks. Protests?

Just in case, I walked back home and grabbed my press badge. And then I headed over to the source of the noise.

Because I was the reporter working that day. So instead of taking time for myself, I gave it to the job I'm thankful to have.

JUNE 1, 2020

Be kind: Give a voice to those who have none

This morning, I called Timothy very early and asked if he would like to go with me to take pictures of last night's damage.

That led to my locating the family of Valle's Produce in Joliet, a little family-run grocery store that suffered heavy vandalism and a fire last night.

Then later that afternoon, as if I didn't have enough to do, the Holy Spirit tapped me on the shoulder and asked me to start calling the black pastors I've interviewed over the years and simply ask their opinions on the recent events.

I called six. One never called me back. One called and asked to talk in the morning.

But the other four spoke as if flood gates were suddenly opened. They were passionate in their feelings, and I tried very hard to write every word they spoke.

I don't walk in their shoes and cannot fully understand their perspectives, although I try my best to empathize and find parallels to further my comprehension.

But nothing will change until we ask the oppressed to speak. And then we must listen with two good ears and one open mind.

JUNE 2, 2020

Be kind: Stretch a little

Having worked straight through the weekend, I was not scheduled for work today.

But I had begun a number of projects I that, I felt, would best be written while the interviews were fresh.

The inconvenience of delaying my personal gratification paled to the horrible situations that others were experiencing.

I finished just before curfew ended and missed my walk, which is good for me in many ways.

But it was one walk. And the stories had potential to help others. So instead of stretching my legs, I stretched my generosity for one night.

JUNE 3, 2020

Be kind: From time to time, say, "yes," to an extra project.

About a decade ago, I interviewed a young pastor of a new church, a former addict who's grown a rather impressively large church and bought an old grocery store to convert into worship space.

Earlier this week, he asked if I could come out to a prayer service that he was hosting in the parking lot. I could have said, "No." And I almost said, "No."

The service was scheduled for Thursday evening. To attend meant skipping out on WriteOn Joliet again.

Yet attending meant writing a story I could easily put together, even while taking photos and shooting video. I felt readers would enjoy it.

As I debated what to do, the pastor texted back. He had the date wrong. It was Wednesday, today. Actually, Thursday was bad for him, a family commitment.

Even though this is not the denomination that most speaks to my spirit, gathering with other believers, even as a member of the press, and hearing prayers and hymns, benefited me more than the extra story.

And yes, readers did enjoy it, too, a double blessing.

JUNE 4, 2020

Be kind: Speak careful words to bless others.

Tonight WriteOn Joliet met. The tone of the meeting reflected the recent events as writers read the pieces they had in their minds and hearts.

I was going to read an excerpt from *Lycanthropic Summer* and then decided against it.

I did, however, share at the very end, since we had time leftover, my blog to the class of 2020.

My sisters two children graduated from college and high school in May, a time that really fell flat for them, as it did for many other graduates.

It was an impulsive decision to share that piece. I received some kind responses, such as, "Have you ever been invited to give a commencement speech?"

Still, I felt going with the tonal flow of the night instead of having "my way" felt like the right decision.

And who knows? Maybe one or two in attendance found something of inspirational value in those carefully crafted words.

It's called, "A Message to the Class of 2020."

You may read it here: bit.ly/2L5poWm.

JUNE 5, 2020

Be kind: Take the time to pursue your form of downtime.

It was actually more convenient, workwise, to work through my free days this past week. But as the days passed, I realized I had more work to finish than I could fit into the week.

Plus, personal tasks were piling up.

The best I could do was move some of it to Sunday, with the resolve to cut some days short the next week.

Then today, I took half a day to play with werewolves. I was productive, out of my day-to-day head for a while, and felt renewed in creativity.

Be kind: Be thankful to those who provide for you.

Today Rebekah, Daniel, and I went to the dentist, a reschedule of our six-month cleanings from back in March.

Our dentist had just reopened on Monday for regular business.

Despite some mutual anxiety and maybe even a little frustration – my hygienist said she'd never worn so much PPE at one time – the visit went well.

In fact, from the first moment she peered into my mouth, she praised my at-home dental care.

The dentist seemed genuinely happy to see me and greeted me with a, "Hello, friend."

While I try to always thank my health care providers, distractions in the moment often cause me to slip up.

Perhaps because these are extraordinary days, I made sure I remembered and expressed sincere appreciation. The risk to them is greater than it is to me.

BTW, I go to New Lenox Dental. They are awesome. Make sure you ask for Dr. Caesar Ciaglia. And tell them I sent you.

Call 815-485-2345 or visit newlenoxdental.com.

JUNE 7, 2020

Be kind: Know when to stop giving.

Today someone really needed to talk. And I gave that person my ear. After an hour, I reminded this person I still had a story for work to write.

Thirty minutes later when that person launched into another story, I crossed a firmer line, letting this person know this was the last story.

So this person kept it going another thirty minutes. After which I said I really had to go. And then that person got miffed. I don't feel badly about it.

I gave a generous amount of time, and I felt good about it. But I could not give that person time that belonged to my job.

JUNE 8, 2020

Be kind: Sometimes the universe is kind to you. Accept it and be happy.

As anyone who's ever gotten stuck in the customer service queue knows, calling to check a balance on a bill is almost never easy and quick.

In this case, the service was last fall, and the last bill I had showed a small balance (thanks to insurance) as well as a large balance (because insurance still hadn't paid on it).

But I hadn't received a bill this month. So before I called the insurance company, I called the provider, a major medical center near Chicago.

I had no balance. And not because of the insurance company.

The small one had been written off. The large one didn't exist.

How about that for a Monday morning blessing?

JUNE 9, 2020

Be kind to the person on the other line. If you listen well, you'll leave blessed.

Today I interviewed an employee for the Cook County sheriff's department who spent five weeks in a local hospital with severe COVID-19.

Hearing the grim details reminded me of how mortally dangerous this virus is. But hearing the story he told after it, a story he might not have told if I hadn't listened well and asked the right questions, really made my day.

The experience inspired him and did the same for me.

Read it here: bit.ly/2UFsL8n.

JUNE 10, 2020

Be kind: Encourage the faint-hearted; be on the same team.

Rebekah approached me today to schedule a time to discuss the design of my personal website, which will also list the skills she's honed to help authors.

It sounds like a simple request, but it is huge for Rebekah. Without going into the details, I'm thrilled at the steps she is taking, especially now that she is unemployed due to COVID-19.

And I let her pick the date and time. And I gave her all the time she needed. She's help me; I'm helping her.

We make a good team.

JUNE 11, 2020

Be kind: Be flexible, especially when others are helping you reach a goal.

I was technically not scheduled to work today. But someone in public relations at a local hospital was working hard to find me sources for a story. All I had to do was interview them.

She got back to me at the end of yesterday. The sources, three of them, were available today.

So I made time to talk to all of them.

This meant I was less productive with the novel I was writing. But why would I do otherwise when she helped me out so much, with a story that is due tomorrow morning?

And being gracious and appreciative by following up was kindness to me, too. After all, as I said, the story is due tomorrow morning.

Seems like a win-win to me, even if I didn't get my way one hundred percent.

JUNE 12, 2020

Be kind: Read June 11. Same principle applies.

I worked this morning, took a walk with Rebekah late morning, and then Rebekah and I had our website meeting, which actually lasted several hours and included some input from Timothy.

I did some editing for clients. I lifted weights. And I haven't looked at fiction at all.

So here I am writing this entry, debating if I should finish my steps or open the novel?

But, honestly, I don't go back to work until Sunday. The problem is not lack of time but how I'm perceiving said time.

I have plenty of time to work on fiction, exercise, and even edit my clients' work.

But if I keep dwelling on the fact that I didn't do such and such at the time I felt drawn to do it, then I'm not making good use of the time I do have.

Being flexible, in this case, is also a kindness to me. I can walk in praise, as Fr. Boris says, or I can sour my time with resentment.

Be kind: Speak difficult words in love.

People tend to communicate challenging messages in two ways: they avoid them or wait until they're angry and spew them.

Neither are useful.

The other day I received the following message from a client whose first draft I'd marked up quite a bit, which is often the case with inexperienced writers and first drafts. Reading through those edits can often cause heart pounding and sensations of suffocation in the writer (I've been there, so I know).

But the only way through it, of course, is through it. Today, I received this lovely message from the client:

Hi Denise, I hope you are having a good weekend. I will be finished with the re-write in a day or two. Let me know when you are ready to start editing again. You did a wonderful job of both editing and educating me. I have grown from the experience. You are the best.

Why is this important? Because when you can deliver the message in love, you also provide an opportunity for the other person to hear the message in love and, as this person said, grow from the experience. And when a writer grows, the gains are immense and really can be applied to any life journey:

- The writer will write a stronger and more-to-the-point draft and, thus, need *less* of an editor's services and spend less time in rewriting, saving both money and time.

- The writer will feel less at the mercy of so-called experts and will know when to defend his/her choice of words, style, construction; when to reflect on feedback; and when to reject another's advice altogether.

A similar instance, and my son Timothy still tells the story, happened with Timothy when he was in his mid-teens.

For years, Timothy's weight had been creeping up, and we'd offered a number of solutions for it: cut back your food (he wouldn't), increase your activity (he didn't), and it's just baby fat (it wasn't).

This was concerning not just for potential issues with self-esteem or practical ones (He was about as wide as he was tall, and he wasn't very tall at all. Finding jeans that fit was impossible with alternations in the length), but also because our family has a strong history of hypertension and diabetes.

One early morning, about 3:30 in the morning when we were out delivering newspapers, we had just turned onto Webster Avenue in Marycrest Subdivision in Joliet, and I was pulling to the curb so he could run out for a porch delivery, when he looked into the side mirror and said, "I'm getting a little chunky."

And I quickly countered, "You're fat."

Maybe the bluntness was due to the earliness of the day and the tight deadline on which we worked. But the upshot was that Timothy got busy. He lost more than sixty pounds over a decade ago and has kept it off.

With the weight loss, he also gained a better attitude and discipline in schoolwork and life goals. If he starts to slip up, he doesn't need reminders from me. He is well able to remind himself.

But "love" is really key. Without love, the speaker becomes a noisy gong of self-importance who is going to tell so and so how wrong he or she is.

Without love, the hearer will become defensive or feel worthless.

Love is more like the red flag waving in "Tootle the Train." Love says, "I hear your goals and I respect them. Here's a way to get back on track."

JUNE 14, 2020

Be kind: Reach out on the behalf of another.

I recently emailed the leader of a major watchdog group for authors that I've followed for more than a decade.

This email was the first I'd ever send to this group.

But I was concerned for another writer that I feared was getting ripped off. I found some information online but not enough that either confirmed my unease or put me at ease.

So I sent the email and received a response that was worse than I anticipated.

And then I did not give the information to the writer, also out of love. The writer had made a commitment to a certain group. Having the knowledge could not undo it.

But I will be ready with plenty of support if the chips fall.

JUNE 15, 2020

Be kind: Look for cues as to when to speak and when to keep silent.

Especially when someone is grieving.
      Especially then.

JUNE 16, 2020

Be kind: When you're entrusted with a job, do your best.

That may sound like commonsense.

But don't think in terms of the minimal. That's not kind to the one for whom you work.

And don't be so hard on yourself that you set a maximum that you can't reach or a maximum that sets you up for neglecting your other responsibilities. That's not kind to you and the others in your life.

As yourself (I ask God, so do that if you believe in God) what this job requires from you and how you can fulfill in an effective way.

And then do it.

JUNE 17, 2020

Be kind: Be flexible, especially in perilous times.

Journalism during a pandemic is a bit all over the place. My duties often change day to day (and even moment to moment) depending what news "breaks" in the world.

Obviously as a person, you can't be all over the place all the time.

But you can be flexible and bend to the circumstances when necessary.

It's really a kindness all the way around.

People who bend don't usually break.

JUNE 18, 2010

Be kind: Step aside for the sake of another.

My WriteOn Joliet co-leader had to bail early for another appointment, so he left me with a flash fiction prompt and the reins of the meeting.

By eight o'clock, we had half an hour left, and everyone had read their pieces except me. However, another member, who hasn't attended often due to his work schedule, had also brought the first draft of his second novel and was hoping to share it with the other attendees.

So I passed on reading mine so he could share his chapter and have time for feedback. And no one even noticed my omission to make an issue of it.

Here's my reasoning: yes, as one of the group, it's important I share, too.

But as a professional writer, I share my non-fiction writings all the time, so much that I often take it for granted that people, in general, pay attention to the pieces I write.

Opportunities to share are leaner for the rest of the group. This time, circumstances made it possible for me to create the opportunity.

So I did. And I believe everyone, the reader and the hearers, were enriched by that decision.

JUNE 19, 2020

Be kind: Talk to your future self.

Today I had a day off, the only day off I've had in a week and the only part of a day off I'll have until next Thursday.

I really wanted to write fiction, but I also had all these editing projects for clients that needed tackling.

On top of that, the concentration for wandering inside my muse would be broken by a few scattered, non-work appointments.

I felt that if I chose fiction, I'd get frustrated with the interruptions and feel stressed this weekend with the undone work.

So I listened to my Saturday and Sunday self and edited work for a client on Friday, promising myself that I'd stay up late and work on some fiction.

And the way my appointments were spaced, the client's work fit nearly in an among the telephone calls. It was a very productive day.

PS: I actually feel asleep early on Friday and woke up early Saturday morning full of ideas for one of my novels in progress. I spent a very fruitful couple of hours before I switched into work duties. Clearly my future self-made the right decision.

JUNE 20, 2020

Be kind: Occasionally give up your downtime for someone who needs your time.

Most of the time, I put a fence around my Saturdays. I need the time to unwind and write fiction.

Even when I'm scheduled to work, I try to leave some "me-time."

This morning, I gave some of that time to the mother of a college-bound teen who needs a kidney. It was the only time she had available to talk.

I can write the story next week. And in the entire scheme of the rest of my life, I lost very little of "me time."

JUNE 21, 2020

Be kind: Be still.

The most peaceful time to take a walk is early Sunday morning.

Most people are not awake, and the world is so quiet and still.

Quiet and still truly does refresh the soul. Try it every now and again.

JUNE 22, 2020

Be kind: Make to-do lists.

Make them for the morning, the afternoon, the day, the week, the month, and the year.

Periodically review them.

Cross off items when you complete them.

Don't you feel more organized, more accomplished?

JUNE 23, 2020

Be kind: Give an opportunity for another.

Do you know someone who needs a knowledge or a skill?
    Introduce that person to someone you know that has it.
    It's a quick double kindness that will leave you feeling good about yourself – which has now become a triple kindness.

JUNE 24, 2020

Be kind: Don't borrow trouble.

A phrase I've occasionally heard from a character in Chinese dramas when another character expresses anxiety about impending challenges: "Why are you worried about that now?"

I'm a planner. I don't like troubles taking me unawares.

So I plan.

But I'm also learning not to fret until the actual moment is there.

Even if I know for certain the next day will bring trouble, I don't have to let the future disturb my sleep in the middle of the night.

JUNE 25, 2020

Be kind: Wash the cat bowls.

That used to be part of our daily routine before we left for the distribution center each morning.

When we washed the breakfast dishes, we washed the cat bowls.

Then we stopped running the newspaper routes in the middle of the night. And the regular washing of the cat bowls stopped, too.

So every now and again, we have to remind ourselves to do it because the habit is lost.

Maybe you don't have a cat or a dog or a goldfish or a parakeet or a houseplant.

But can you feed a bird? A stray cat? Buy a bag of dog food for an animal rescue?

JUNE 26, 2020

Be kind: Listen with an open mind to a perspective that isn't yours.

COVID-19 and racism.

The first is a topic that didn't exist in our lives twelve months ago.

The second is a topic many people thought was resolved a long time ago.

Quite a few people have opinions on both. A great deal of people express those opinions loudly and/or on social media.

Except at home, I haven't really shared my opinions on either.

But I've spent a lot of time listening to the opinions of others.

It's really the only way to arrive at a resolution of both.

JUNE 27, 2020

Be kind: Revel in smallish treats.

Before the pandemic, Rebekah and I would get up early on Saturday morning, go across the street for coffee (me) and tea (her), and then go for a walk.

Later in the morning, Timothy would often ask if I'd like to take a drive for coffee. We'd often end up at Louis Joliet Mall at the Gloria Jean's kiosk.

Those routines are gone. But lately, on Saturdays, Timothy and Daniel get up early and come back with Dunkin coffee for me and them and tea for Rebekah.

It's not just the beverages that make me feel warm inside.

JUNE 28, 2020

Be kind: Ride the extra miles.

Although it's a day of rest for many people, I worked an extra-long day today in order to ride to Loyola on Tuesday with Timothy (the driver) and Rebekah (the patient).

Rebekah is afraid of doctors, and she will have to fly solo on her first visit to my endocrinologist. But I can be outside, nearby, cheering her on.

JUNE 29, 2020

Be kind: Notice shapes and colors.

Remember when you were a child, and you saw animals in clouds and sidewalk cracks?

Rebekah still sees them (occasionally, I do, too) and points them out to me, so I can also see and enjoy them.

Life will seem kinder and gentler when you see the subtleties many miss.

In turn, you may treat others with greater kindness and gentleness.

Be kind: Make a cheat sheet.

Here's a great idea that's a kindness to you and your doctor.

I made Rebekah a cheat sheet for the endocrinologist.

Rebekah is very shy and struggles with organizing her thoughts and communicating. So I wrote that first on her sheet.

Then I included her medical history, her symptoms, and the reason for the visit – all in concise bullet points.

This way, the endocrinologist had a snapshot of the issue and could be sweet and reassuring to Rebekah. In turn, Rebekah felt very comfortable answering questions since she didn't have to organize a backlog of information in her mind.

Heck, I'm going to make one for myself.

JULY 1, 2020

Be kind: Enjoy the talents of others.

Tonight I watched a Zoom performance of Oscar Wilde's "A Woman of No Importance," which my niece and goddaughter Rachel played a role and directed.

I logged on to be supportive.

And wound up being entertained and impressed.

I was entertained by the talents of the actors.

And I was impressed at the creativity involved in creating an enjoyable piece of virtual theater.

Be kind: Celebrate freedom of speech.

But how to celebrate it?

The Bible offers this advice: "Let your conversation be always full of grace, seasoned with salt, so that you may know how to answer everyone." Colossians 4:6

Socrates offers this: "Is it true; is it kind, or is it necessary?"

Epictetus says: "We have two ears and one mouth so that we can listen twice as much as we speak."

The Bible also says this: "A man of knowledge restrains his words, and a man of understanding maintains a calm spirit. Even a fool is considered wise if he keeps silent, and discerning when he holds his tongue." Proverbs 17: 27-28

The educator A.S. Neill would make the case for "freedom" and not "license."

How can we use this freedom and be kind at the same time?

JULY 3, 2020

Be kind: Love yourself.

Every now and again, make time to quietly pursue the pursuits that appeal to you – if only to remind yourself you have the freedom to do so.

Being kind to others when you're resentful at losing your personal time is not true kindness – especially if losing your personal time has become a habit.

Sure, the kind act is often a great inconvenience to us, and we may be often called to place ourselves last for the good of another.

But just remember you are "another" too. And, sometimes, put your needs first.

JULY 4, 2020

Be kind: Celebrate freedom.

My new neighbors celebrated their freedom starting at eleven o'clock tonight.

They decided to shoot off stadium-style fireworks outside my window, even letting their four-year-old child help.

I can't even begin to explain how that noise resounded through my chest or the skipped heartbeats and chest pain it caused.

The police never showed up until nearly dawn to break up the party. But I imagine the police were quite busy all night. This pandemic year was the worst for fireworks I've ever experienced, and those fireworks started last month.

Most nights, I could ignore them and eventually fall asleep. But not last night.

But I could choose not to be angry about it. However, that took all of my effort and energy.

I even prayed for the neighbors, too.

But I fought resentment and unkind thoughts at every syllable.

But that's how I chose to celebrate my freedom.

JULY 5, 2020

Be kind: Clean up someone else's mess.

So the mess from our neighbors Fourth of July party meant the street all the way into the intersection and a main traffic light was full of garbage and broken glass.

Timothy and Rebekah spent an hour outside in the heat today cleaning up the mess.

They were concerned that innocent drivers might experience blow-outs from all the glass.

That's how they celebrated their freedom. Tired as they were from being up all night while the neighbors partied in front of our house, they chose kindness toward the other neighbors.

JULY 6, 2020

Be kind: When energy is low, rely on will.

Needless to say, I am tired and a little cranky today.

But I am making a huge effort to be sweet and kind.

I don't feel like it. But I want to feel like it. So I am trying really hard.

Besides, why should the people I encounter today bear the brunt of my sleepiness and stress?

Be kind: Celebrates the haves and the haves not.

When my oldest child was a toddler and money was super tight, I added more celebration to our lives.

One of those celebrations included celebrating half birthdays, typically with half a cake and singing half of the "birthday song."

Now that the kids are older, I often forget to wish them a happy half birthday – and they miss that.

Rebekah especially has the worst luck with her birthday and half birthday. Her birthday is on Old Calendar Christmas, so she often feels it gets lost among the other festivities.

Six months later, her half birthday gets lost in other people's work obligations, since most of us are not working on Independence Day and are back to work on July 7.

So today I wanted to surprise her with a vintage activity: playing jacks. I had the jacks and no ball. In a non-COVID year, we would have walked to Walmart and browsed the store. This year, I don't shop in stores, and Rebekah doesn't browse.

But she was happy I remembered her day. And I owe her a game of jacks.

Be kind: Use magic words.

My parents took my sister and me to Florida the Easter I was in second grade.

I had an awe-inspiring swim in the Gulf of Mexico. And we visited a circus. At one point, a man with a skeleton marionette did a routine and decided to call a child onstage with him.

I'm rarely chosen for anything, but I was picked for this. So down to the stage I went. I remember very little about the skit except two things.

One was being encouraged to give the marionette a kiss on its pink cheek, which immediately flustered the puppet into a jumble of string and bones.

So the skeleton said the only way to put him back together was to say a magic word; did I know any?

Well, it just so happens, my sister had a record called "Let's Play School." On that record was a song about using these magic words: May I? Please. Thank you.

So I said a very sincere, "Please." And that caused a bit of a pause from the puppet and its puppet master.

But the puppet master quickly recovered and instructed to the audience to shout "Please!" at the count of three. We all did, and the marionette jumped back together.

My parents gave me some strange looks when I returned to my seat on the bleachers.

But I still believe "may I," "please," and "thank you" are the best kind of magic words one can utter.

JULY 9, 2020

Be kind: Take a moment to pray or think good thoughts about someone else.

We tend to pray when we need something.

How about taking a moment right now and pray for someone else's needs?

JULY 10, 2020

Be kind: Let the inner child out from time to time

My former publicist once told me I was in touch with my inner three-year-old. It was a compliment, and I accepted it.

I still get excited on Friday nights. Hurray! I can stay up late!

I like to get a waffle cone with soft serve ice cream and hard chocolate topping once during the summer.

Christmas, with all its beautiful decorations, colored lights, and mysteriously wrapped packages is the most magical time of the year.

My favorite Halloween costume is a witch, and I dress up as one every year.

I still want dolls for Christmases and birthdays.

There are two benefits to this.

You won't grow old in spirit.

And others will feel comfortable growing young with you.

Be kind: Invite others to create with you

Do you like to create? Invite another to create with you.

Last year, my WriteOn Joliet co-leader Tom Hernandez suggested members pair up to co-create. I was paired with three other members, and the resulting works were greater than our individual creative limitations. We displayed our works at the downtown branch of the Joliet Public Library for a month.

Last year, another member invited Rebekah and me to make scroll journals with her.

For the last couple of years, Timothy and I have collaborated to write books in the middle grade series The Adventures of Cornell Dyer.

I collaborate with local artists for covers and illustrations for my books.

I have friends who used to host monthly "art nights."

This year has opened up new opportunities for collaboration, too.

Try it, even if you don't think you're very creative or artistic. It might help you release your inner child (see the July 10 entry), who freely creates without worrying if the result is "good enough."

How can inviting someone to create with you be a kindness?

Because many people also feel inhibited with creating. By inviting someone to create with you, you're inviting that person to journey with you through the messy process of not being perfect and "on."

Many people never receive an invitation like it.

JULY 12, 2020

Be kind: Buy into another's dreams, part one.

.

So when I met with Ed Calkins in January, we scheduled another meeting for today (his request) to keep him accountable and on track with his first novel.

Because of the pandemic, we talked by phone today instead.

The real Ed Calkins is a former supervisor from my newspaper delivery days. He's a writer that gave up writing years ago due to his severe dyslexia.

But Ed is very creative and created an alter ego of himself. Legally and with his permission, I fictionalized this character in my BryonySeries.

And then I invited him to blog on my blog. A couple years ago, I took a collection of his blogs, published them, and set up a book signing for him.

I did it without his knowledge. He was stunned and said, "I've always dreamed of publishing something."

Last year, a fan of my series asked me to write Ed's back story. I felt only Ed could do that. He said he'd think about it.

Then one day, he abruptly sent me several hilarious chapters with the request, "Should I keep going?"

Of course!

Then he wanted to know what I would charge for editing his novel. Well, nothing.

Here's the way I see it. I know, and Ed knows, my books and his books aren't going to rock the world. But that doesn't mean no one will read them. And it also doesn't mean I can't use my experience with self-publishing to give him a traditional publishing experience.

It's costing me nothing but time. And what better way to spend one's time than by helping another person make his dream come true.

JULY 13, 2020

Be kind: Buy into another's dreams, part two.

When COVID began, several incidents happened at once.

My insurance stopped paying for my medicine, forcing me to either switch to a new medication or pay full price for the current one. Because this medicine has kept me asthma-free since 2007, I opted for the latter.

Shortly afterwards, I had a temporary reduction in work hours.

Several writers, some of whom were laid off from their jobs, approached me about editing their novels.

I had already said "yes" to one novelist last year and had completed a couple rounds of his manuscript. I decided to say "yes" to a few more.

Most of the reasoning for turning down extra jobs in past years is because I had no extra hours. I now had those hours, for a couple of months anyway. So why not use that extra time to help writers with their goals?

JULY 14, 2020

Be kind: Be humble and grateful when others work for your benefit.

I always had bikes as a child but never a blue bike (blue is my favorite color).

So when I bought bikes for my family after we moved near the I&M Canal in Channahon, my husband Ron made sure the bike he bought for me was blue.

That was the fall of 1999. I still have the bike.

By now the parts were worn and rusty. But while I was upstairs working today, Timothy and Daniel refurbished the bike.

They also had some stories to tell about the scarcity of bike parts during a pandemic and the effort they made to track them down.

Tomorrow is my birthday. They rushed like mad to surprise me with a re-made blue bike.

When it came time to unveil it, I refused to come down. I was off tomorrow (again, my birthday) and needed to finish up work.

But they persisted. So I went downstairs. And then – ta-da!

I, of course, was surprised and thrilled. But the happiness is less about the blue bike and more about the kind of men my sons had become.

They are the type of men who will spend hours seeking parts and then refurbishing an old blue bike for their mother.

JULY 15, 2020

Be kind: Take the time to reply to every birthday greeting on social media.

My feeling is this: if someone took the time to send me a greeting, I can take the time to reply to it.

So most of my birthday is spent replying to birthday messages on social media.

No, this isn't a waste of time. Perhaps someday I'll be so old and forgotten that no one takes the time to greet me.

Today, I am grateful and blessed.

JULY 16, 2020

Be kind: Honor the effort, especially when that effort was made in your direction.

Jasmine was disappointed because she could only drop off either my cake or Riley's cake yesterday.

Riley is my granddaughter. We share a birthday and a middle name because my daughter-in-law Amber is kind and loving. She picked the name and scheduled her C/section on my birthday. It was one of her first thoughts when she found out her due date.

Because of COVID, Riley and I virtually shared out birthdays. And Jasmine (Timothy's girlfriend who bakes all our cakes), had two cakes that had to go in opposite directions.

A major thunderstorm was brewing. We exhorted her to go to Riley's house and stop by my house tomorrow.

Jasmine did. And some of the frosting on my BryonySeries cake had melted in the heat. She was super disappointed. I was not and thanked her profusely.

She put a lot of love in every crumb. Love, even love that's smudged a little, is better than no love.

JULY 17, 2020

Be kind: Be thankful for new opportunities during terrible days.

What good are you doing this year that you might not have done, if not for the pandemic?

Be thankful for it.

And continue seeking out those new opportunities.

JULY 18, 2020

Be kind: Be grateful and amazed for unorthodox solutions.

That's it.

What a marvelous way to renew your sense of wonder in a challenging year.

Now pass on the blessing.

JULY 19, 2020

Be kind: Accept the kindness of others.

Most of us would rather be givers than receivers.

In fact, it can feel downright awkward to receive. Maybe it makes us feel selfish.

But it's an unkindness to deprive another the opportunity to give.

And now you have insight to the feelings of receivers when you give.

This insight will make you a better giver.

JULY 20, 2020

Be kind: Help a tiny life.

Today a woman from across the street called out to Rebekah and me.

She had found a baby bird and didn't know what to do.

So while she waited, I contacted some people I knew from wildlife rescues who were happy to talk with her and guide her.

A few minutes of time and resources shared provided kindness in so many directions.

Some of my expert acquaintances now know I consider them to be experts.

These experts had the opportunity to share their knowledge.

A stranger made some new connections and learned some new skills.

A baby bird had a new chance at life.

JULY 21, 2020

Be kind: Step out in trust.

Except for walks, I've gone nowhere during this entire pandemic.

Today, I decided to test the public health guidelines. I masked up and went to Hobby Lobby to help Timothy pick out frames for some artwork I need framed and hung.

The hour was early, and the store was nearly empty, so the jaunt was low risk.

We should not put our trust into sand, of course. Blind trust benefits no one.

But if the precepts are true, and we are wary, well, which is sand?

JULY 22, 2020

Be kind: Forgive yourself when you're unkind.

Sometimes we're just too tried, too hungry, too annoyed, and too selfish to be kind.

Forgive yourself.

JULY 23, 2020

Be kind: Give a new life to an old cat.

Senior cats often live the rest of their lives in shelters because they aren't as cute as kittens.

But senior cats are often the least troublesome pet companions. They are quiet and like to sleep. They aren't overly eager for affection.

They just need care.

Several senior cats keep popping back up when I put together the weekly "Pets of the Week" for The Herald-News.

Someone finally adopted George from the Will County Humane Society in Shorewood (I did write some stories to help, but those were a long time ago), but Max is still there.

Spunk and Biscuit from Humane Haven Animal Shelter in Bolingbrook still don't have homes after quite a few years.

In fact, Rebekah said that when our cats die, she's going to adopt Spunk and Biscuit.

But even though our cats are now senior cats, they are fairly healthy. So please beat Rebekah to the adoption.

Or please adopt Max.

Visit willcountyhumane.com or hhhas.org for more information.

JULY 24, 2020

Be kind: Schedule time to be kind

Every act of kindness doesn't have to be spontaneous. In fact, if we don't schedule it sometimes, it doesn't happen.

Schedule a phone call with a friend instead of playing phone tag.

Schedule a virtual coffee date with a relative instead of waiting for the pandemic to be done.

Schedule a time to pamper yourself instead of putting it off because you're too tired.

Be kind: Give a rock a home.

Do you collect rocks? I do.

Not formally, no.

But ever since I was a child, I've brought home rocks that appealed to me: smooth rocks, rocks with faces, rocks with colors, etc.

My kids, when they were small, did the same for me. When we moved to Channahon, they brought me little shells from the canal, too, enough to fill pretty jars (with shells and rocks) and set them around the house.

Timothy painted a rock for me at a home-school cooperative, and I carried it in my pocket for a long time.

My grandfather used to polish rocks and give them to my sister and me as gifts. I "saw" many beautiful underwater or aquarium scenes in them.

Today WriteOn Joliet resumed its Author of the Month program at The Book Market in Crest Hill.

Our featured author Holly Coop had a basket of painted kindness rocks – complimentary gifts for the bookstore's patrons.

Holly invited me to take a rock, so I looked for the perfect one.

You see, Rebekah is going through some challenges. So I selected the right rock for her and gifted her with it today.

Holly writes inspirational poetry. Her website is at hollycoopbooks.com.

JULY 26, 2020

Be kind: Give yourself a wide berth to do a project right.

Even though Sunday is considered a day of rest, I have worked every Sunday for many years.

For more than a dozen of those years, I delivered newspapers with my family, seven days a week, in the middle of the night. "Sunday" didn't begin until the last newspaper went out of the window (or onto the porch). Then we went home, changed into "Sunday" clothes, and headed up to church, forty-five minutes away.

After we started the youth group, we often had three vehicles on the road, driving to five different towns to pick up other kids for church, too.

Once there, I ran a Sunday School and taught two of its grades. Ron and I sat on the church board. Once a month, we also cooked a dinner for the parish, paying for it out of our money. Ron also painted walls and waxed floors.

When we got home, I set up the next week's lessons for all the Sunday School classes and repacked all the Sunday School boxes. My mind was in Sunday School mode, and it was more efficient that way.

When I became an employee, I started working Sunday afternoons to get a jump on the work week. I started this after my assistant left for another job. It helped relieve the anxiety I felt on Monday mornings.

Over the past couple of years, I've written my "An Extraordinary Life" stories on Sundays. Because of the sensitive nature of these stories, I like taking time away from the time pressure of the work week and simply focus on them. I feel I write a better story that way.

Sometimes, to give certain projects the attention they deserve, we have to give them the time they deserve.

How is this kind?

Well, you'll be less stressed. The project will turn out well. And if the project is meant for someone else, that person will receive the fruits of your very best efforts.

JULY 27, 2020

Be kind: Share time with another.

I like to walk early in the morning. Since Rebekah has been out of worked, we have walked together.

Walking is usually my listening to music, let-my-mind-wander time. This year has been creatively challenging because I've given that time in the morning to Rebekah, and I'd given that time in evening back in the spring to Timothy.

But some day I won't have that time to give.

And someday, my kids will be gone and won't want to spend that time with me.

So I've looked for other ways to free my mind because I need that, too.

And I've reveled in this pandemic blessing with two of my kids.

Be kind: Even through gritted teeth.

Do you know someone in your life who triggers emotions that are not kind, at least some of the time?

I do.

And sometimes, I just really want to teach them a lesson.

And there's nothing wrong with that.

Just be sure you teach them the right lesson.

You know what I mean.

Besides, you'll be teaching two people the right lesson.

That person.

And you.

JULY 29, 2020

Be kind: Staycation gracefully.

I really look forward to going to Raleigh every August.

My oldest daughter's husband was transferred there a decade ago.

But until I was working as an employee for a year and a half, I didn't have the time or money to visit her – until 2015, 2016, and 2017.

In 2018, airfare jumped, and the price was out of my budget. So I took an at-home writing retreat instead. And then I went to Raleigh in 2019. However, I'd enjoyed the at-home writing retreat so much, I was a bit disappointed that I couldn't take an at-home writing retreat and a trip to Raleigh.

This year, I'm taking two of them. The first is next month.

We can't always have everything we want when we want to have it.

But if we want a good thing, the right time for having it may appear.

When it does, be gracious and accept it. The opportunity is always more fruitful than wishful thinking.

You'll be happier and that happiness will encourage others to be happy in their present circumstances, too.

JULY 30, 2020

Be kind: Inspire.

My first post on Facebook each day is a Bible verse.

As a Christian who's paid to write, I feel my first words of the day should be God's words.

What's crazy is that I've had people come up to me through the years who tell me they stop by my page each day for that reason.

These are people who don't "like" the post. But they do share how the post has inspired them.

It's such a small act. But it has such a wide outreach.

JULY 31, 2020

Be kind: Be pleasant.

Here are a few suggestions for making pleasant moments.

Say good morning on social media.

Thank people for performing a service for you, even if that service is their jobs.

Ask people how they are today and really listen.

Look people in the eye and smile at them. This way, they know you've seen them and that you like what you see.

Because, you see, some people can't bear the sight of their own reflection.

But maybe your acceptance of them will go a long way toward them accepting themselves.

AUGUST 1, 2020

Be kind: Be present and safe.

Be present to others in the moment even if you can't be physically present.

And be safe.

During a worldwide pandemic, being safe is a kindness to you and a kindness to them.

AUGUST 2, 2020

Be kind: Step over the line.

It's good to set boundaries on our time, or others will it for us.

Occasionally, I let that line be crossed for a greater good.

Recently I wrote a story on a man who had recently died. A long list of friends wanted to share their stories and memories. The only way to get talk to them all was to make myself available to random phone calls when I wasn't available.

I could have said, "No." I sometimes do when too many sources detracts from the story.

But each person added another layer of knowledge and connection, and I'm glad I took this approach.

Obviously, it's not good for any of us to always be "on." Sometimes, the greater kindness is to say, "No."

But sometimes, the greater kindness is to make an exception and say, "Yes."

Be kind: Develop an old relationship.

A few years ago, I picked up the phone and called my uncle. We were not on bad terms. But we were not on good terms. In fact, we were not on any terms.

He had always lived out of state. Every four years or so (when I was a child), he and his family (my cousins) visited us. Once, we went to see them.

Most of that fell apart when my cousins and I became adults. So one day, out of nowhere, I decided to change that. It's taken time to develop the relationship. And I thought he might faint the first time I told him, "I love you."

But we've since supported each other through a mutual relative's illness. Since the time we reconnected, his wife became ill, was diagnosed with cancer, and has died. We talked through all of that.

We've even had lunch one, in person, about six months before the pandemic, when he was in town. He's talked to my kids on the phone independent of me, kids he met only a couple times when they were children.

Maybe you have someone in your life you'd like to know better.

AUGUST 4, 2020

Be kind: Celebrate growth – yours and theirs.

Did you cross three of the five items off your to-do list today?

Have you lost three of the twenty pounds you've set as a goal?

Did you break up a squabble between your preschoolers without raising your voice?

Were you able to shrug off the driver who cut you off today?

Or are you down on yourself – and others – for the targets you – and they – failed to meet?

Try giving yourself a mental "high-five" for the parts you got right and then resolve to build on your success tomorrow.

Be kind: Appreciate the service of others.

Rebekah often forgets to give the cats fresh water, so I usually handle that. But she does keep an eye on certain aspects of their well-being – like Frances, a senior inside cat who wound up with an infected paw, which Rebekah brought to my attention.

It would never have occurred to me to check the paws of any of the cats.

So into the vet went the cat for antibiotics, a process we repeated three times before the infection finally cleared up. In the meantime, Frances had X-rays and bloodwork to rule out any other issues (like a tumor) that might be causing the issue.

And Rebekah kept an eye on the paw during all of this.

Now I did brainstorm with the vet for the treatment that finally cleared up the infection. But that's my service and talent.

Which I doubt Frances appreciated.

Don't be like Frances.

Keep your paws healthy and appreciate the people who care for you.

AUGUST 6, 2020

Be kind: Let another lead you.

Even better: Don't just "let" someone lead, as if you're doing that person a huge favor.

Tell (or show) that person how their leadership impacted you. So what if the impact isn't huge to the world if it's huge to you?

For instance, my WriteOn Joliet co-leader Tom Hernandez likes to offer a "flash fiction" variation to our regular critique meeting from time to time.

We had one tonight. And I wrote every prompt with a werewolf theme as if the main character in my upcoming novel *Lycanthropic Summer* was writing these werewolf miniature stories.

I like the way they turned out. I like this new addition to a nearly finished novel. It never occurred to me to add this element.

And I'm thankful to Tom for providing the opportunity.

By the way, his website is at tomhernandezbooks.com.

Be kind: Be patient when communication breaks down.

I'm not good at a lot of things. But I am good at figuring out ways to get through a communication snarl.

One of my sons was having trouble explaining an issue to his pulmonologist's nurse. So I called and talked to her. It took some back and forth until she understood. But I had the insight to see where she wasn't understanding. So I kept reframing the message until the "aha!" light bulb went on.

Let's face it. Communication often breaks down, and I'm the first one to go, "Duh?" because I can be rather dense at understanding certain concepts.

So it's important to be patient with others when they don't understand us the first (or eighth) time either.

AUGUST 8, 2020

Be kind: Be present in the moment.

Just me and the words.

  Or just you and the puzzles.

  Or just you and the garden.

  Whatever it is, be kind and enjoy the gift of full enjoyment of you and your interests. Don't spoil the moment with distracted or anxious thinking.

AUGUST 9, 2020

Be kind: Rest someone's mind.

I often hear the following question when I interview someone for a story that will be published in The Herald-News: "Can you send me a copy before you publish it?"

The answer is always, "no," for reasons too detailed to explain here.

But I can call back to double-check facts and read back quotes.

I understand why they ask. No one wants to be misquoted or sound "stupid" in print. (I hear that a lot: "Please don't make me sound stupid").

It does take a few minutes to make that call and check those facts, and I don't have to do that most of the time.

But taking a couple extra minutes to allay a person's fears is not a bad use of anyone's time.

AUGUST 10, 2020

Be kind: Be thankful for the luxuries we take for granted.

A derecho blew through Will County this afternoon.

Shortly afterwards, I was wandering through rubble, taking pictures of the aftermath for The Herald-News

This single, brief storm uprooted trees, damaged homes and properties, and cut power to thousands of homes. Many people were especially angry about the loss of power and internet.

Offering prayers and thinking good thoughts for the safety of the workers who bring us such luxuries as refrigerators and hot water might be a better use of time while we're eating crackers in the dark than griping.

AUGUST 11, 2020

Be kind: Don't trample on the rights of another.

Today I wrote a story about a toddler with cancer who nearly missed his second birthday celebration because of unrest in the city where he was receiving treatment.

I believe people must stand up for themselves and for what is right.

But when I do, and when you do, we must be careful not to do unto others what we don't want done unto us.

AUGUST 12, 2020

Be kind: Be thankful for technological blessings.

Today I'm thankful for mobile hotspots that gave me internet connection to do my job after a derecho knocked out the electricity and internet in Will County.

My power is back on. My internet is out. But I am not losing work time or missing deadlines because I have a piece of technology beside me that is keeping things humming. And being thankful for it is a kindness.

Why?

Because my disposition remained sweet in the midst of the challenges. That blessed me – and anyone I encountered today.

AUGUST 13, 2020

Be kind: Share, fully share, the interest of another.

A few years ago, I began watching Asian dramas that Rebekah curated for me because she no longer had friends that shared her interest in Asian culture and entertainment.

Although I began watching to support my daughter, I never thought I'd look forward to watching them with her. And we've watched quite a few in 2020.

A simple act of kindness turned into a win-win-win for us.

She had companionship, and I had a new interest, which can only positively impact my writing, too.

AUGUST 14, 2020

Be kind: Spotlight someone else's good works.

An injured baby squirrel will live another day because a kind person picked it up after the derecho and found a local squirrel rescue to accept it.

That might not sound like a big deal to you.

But you are not a squirrel.

Yes, I wrote a story about it. And I'm glad I did. Because I added a postscript to this post.

A few weeks later, someone I know in another state rescued two baby squirrels and didn't know what to do.

By connecting the novice with the expert, two more squirrels are now doing well.

AUGUST 15, 2020

Be kind: A kindness from you may cause of ripples of more kindness.

I've written a series of stories about a Joliet toddler who has cancer.

The stories have made regional news, enough that major news stations have now featured the child and his family.

And those stories have gone viral across social media – which sent a flood of donations to his donation page.

Most of us want to be a big fish, even if we don't admit it. But we don't need to be a big fish to make a big difference. A small ripple become part of a giant wave.

AUGUST 16, 2020

Be kind: Give up something of yours to someone who has less.

Today I interviewed a North Carolina girl who gave up her birthday (i.e. the money for her cakes, presents, etc.) to donate those dollars to the Joliet toddler who has cancer.

It's easy to give up what we don't really need.

It's harder to give up something we really want or need.

This little girl reminded me of the value of real giving.

AUGUST 17, 2020

Be kind: Be respectful and sweet to people who induce the opposite in you.

Ever wind up on the phone with a customer service representative for (insert name here) that just give you the run around?

My initial reaction is to inwardly fume about how such rudeness could have cost my job when I was a newspaper carrier.

But such an attitude, which will spill out in my tone of voice, won't get me better service.

Of course, being sweet and respectful doesn't necessarily work, either. But being sweet and respectful should not be a tactic. It should be part of my character.

And that character is tested when people stir up the opposite feelings. But good character might be weak character if it can't stand a little heat.

Be persistent in getting your needs met. But be kind.

AUGUST 18, 2020

Be kind: Be open to new routines.

When I was a freelance writer, I used to power walk around the baseball field across the street from my house right after I was through delivering the route.

It was a convenient way to exercise since my neighborhood had no sidewalks, and the sun had not yet risen when I returned home.

But when deadlines grew later, my ending time ran into the time one of my editors started work. So I would make my immediate writing deadlines and break before lunch for a power walk.

When The Herald-News hired me, I shifted those walks to before work. If the day went sideways, I had taken care of me first.

Since Rebekah has been out of work with the pandemic, we've been walking together. This is different for me as I like being a solitary walker. So I do my "alone" walking at night as Timothy is now walking with Daniel in evening.

By pairing up with Rebekah, I've supported her efforts to form new habits, a kindness to her – and to me.

I'm learning to become less rigid in my habits.

AUGUST 19, 2020

Be kind: Draw attention to an unnoticed blessing.

I recently received a news release to a time capsule that was buried at the soon-to-be opened new courthouse for Will County.

But when I read the release, I saw the amount of work that went into creating that time capsule. The items in the time capsule were from Will County students; multiple schools and grade levels participated.

So I decided to put some time into writing a bigger story.

However, if I had not taken the time to read deeper into the words and notice the months of labor to make it happen, I would have failed to acknowledge the efforts – and readers might have blipped over the project, too.

Some kindnesses are not automatically apparent at first glance, especially such a multi-level one as this time capsule.

What a gift the future will receive when the capsule is brought out of the ground in a few decades.

AUGUST 20, 2020

Be kind: Be aware of the struggles of others.

Some of the members of WriteOn Joliet are tired of virtual meetings. I am not, and neither are members who have moved out of state and can't attend in-person anymore.

But I don't represent the entire group. So my co-leader and I are working out a plan to host some hybrid meetings.

Remember your experience is not the same as another's. Try to see the need from another perspective and do your best to hear and meet it.

AUGUST 21, 2020

Be kind: stand up for your safety and the safety of others.

Today a workman came into our home without a mask. I had to insist he wear one. This was not easy to do because we did not speak the same language.

He also insisted on walking through the house to go out a different door. He came back with the mask and went into the upstairs bathroom to get the work done and shut the door.

You know that gut instinct?

I went upstairs and knocked on the door. He opened it – with the mask off. I made an issue of it and called our management company.

The workman's boss knocked on my front door a few minutes later (wearing a mask) and asked for him. They both left.

When the workman returned, he had the mask on. And he kept it on.

I tried to explain to him as best I could that it was for his protection, too.

I understand different people have different understandings and opinions about the whole facemask issue.

But in my home, please respect mine.

AUGUST 22, 2020

Be kind: Retreat.

For introverts like me, retreating sounds amazing.

But I'm embarking on an at-home writing retreat. I've done a few these. And they are not amazing.

They are intense and frustrating and mentally taxing.

But some projects are best flogged out in quietness and solitude.

This week, I'll have both.

The amazing part will come later when I reread the parts that I'll write this week.

Most of that writing will be awful.

But some will be amazing and worth refining.

If you have a project you keep putting off, schedule some retreat time for yourself, too.

AUGUST 23, 2020

Be kind: Connect even when connecting isn't the same.

Virtual birthdays are not the same as JSOHAUD.

Does that make sense to you? Me, neither.

I have no idea why those letters are there, and I only noticed them when I was scrolling back through the entries. But you know what? Virtual birthdays aren't like JSOHAUD – and they aren't like in-person ones either.

But they sure as heck beat zero birthdays and no connection.

Today is the birthday of my third child, Joshua Paul.

Joshua is the handiest handyman I know. He can paint, roof, mud and tape, remodel, and frame-up a building.

He is also very brave. He's battled ill health for nearly a decade (not every illness has yet been identified). He's worked long and hard hours through most of it, and most of it was spent raising a family in poverty. Every challenge was twenty times the challenge it might have been for most people. Yet, Joshua just pragmatically rolled up his sleeves and kept going.

He's an excellent housekeeper. Need laundry done and folded neatly? He's your man. He can wash mountains of dishes quickly while keeping good sanitation principles. He can cook, clean, and organize like no other.

Just so you know.

AUGUST 24, 2020

Be kind: Unpack.

I'm not just unpacking ideas this week at my first at-home writing retreat of 2020.

I'm unpacking boxes from my family's move in 2013. And we've moved three more times since then.

My schedule is overall tight, so when I get free time, I don't want to spend it unpacking boxes.

But since I'm on retreat, Rebekah and I decided to unpack one box a day before I start writing. By the end of the retreat, I'll be done.

Maybe you're storing some things that need unpacking. A little at a time is a good way to tackle it.

AUGUST 25, 2020

Be kind: Set goals and stick to them.

To stay on track and to not exhaust and discourage myself, I have writing goals for each day.

I had a very productive weekend, so I've already modified them.

But I'm realistic to know some days will be less productive.

Be kind to yourself and try to focus on the overall goal.

AUGUST 26, 2020

Be kind: Stretch yourself.

Sometimes people waver between two extremes with their goals: procrastination and overextension.

In the middle is a bit of a stretch. Thinking of reaching on tip toes to grab something off a shelf.

Be kind to yourself today. Do something to stretch yourself just a bit in whatever goal is important to you.

For me on an at-home writing retreat, it means pushing my mind a little more when ideas and words dry up.

AUGUST 27, 2020

Be kind: Know when to push, know when to stop.

It's an intense fiction writing week. Some people might think creative writing is easier than features writing. Both have their own level of difficulty.

Here's where features has a distinct edge: I gather the information and then I write it in a (hopefully) compelling fashion.

With fiction, I must make it all up. I must invent whole people in believable worlds with distinct personalities and needs and feelings and goals and wishes. I must give them distinct speech patterns on the page that represents their individuality.

By the time this writing retreat is up, I'll have spent more than one hundred hours and written tens of thousands of words that will all need editing.

I will have spent more than a hundred hours writing very bad writing.

So when my brain goes from chugging to gasping for air, it's time to take a break.

Sure, sometimes a muse only needs coaxing (or stretching, as the previous post said). And sometimes the muse is simply exhausted.

Too many times we beat ourselves up when we don't make our goals.

But maybe the goals were impossible.

Or maybe they're possible but not just all at once.

Here's the thing: celebrate the accomplishment and forgive what couldn't be done for now.

Don't be a quitter. But do know when to take a break.

AUGUST 28, 2020

Be kind: Break bread.

Have you ever made homemade bread? There's really nothing like it.

In the nearly two decades that I was a stay-at-home mom whose job was taking care of the kids (including home-schooling them) and the house, we made homemade bread nearly every day. And I taught them how to make bread, too.

We had family meals for most of our three meals each day. And we literally broke bread together, using the bread we had made together.

Have no time or interest in making bread? That's OK.

Share a meal or even cup of coffee with someone you love.

If we can't make even fifteen minutes to enjoy the company of someone we love, we need to take another look at how we spend our lives.

AUGUST 29, 2020

Be kind: Wind down.

Today is the official last full day of my first staycation writing retreat of 2020. My brain is tired, and I'm giving it a chance to wind down.

Yes, I'm writing, but I'm being realistic in my writing. The goal was to give myself a workable first draft in the remaining chapters of a novel-in-progress.

I accomplished it, but none of the prose will win any awards, that's for sure.

But I've pushed my mind hard this week. And even minds need a break.

Whether it's been a tough day at work or a tough week at home, remember to be kind to your mind.

Pamper it a bit. Let is rest and relax.

It will reward you the next day.

AUGUST 30, 2020

Be kind: Get ahead of Monday morning.

Since I was out from work all week with a staycation writing retreat, I helped out my Monday morning self by taking a couple hours on Sunday to catch up on email.

It was a gentle way to ease myself back into my work frame of mind without losing the whole day off.

I tend to do some work on Sundays anyway. And it makes Mondays so much easier.

AUGUST 31, 2020

Be kind: Take the journey with another.

Is someone you know going through something tough?

Walk with them for part of the journey.

If you're inclined to send one text, send two.

Be present in real time, even if being present can only be virtual.

If you can give just five minutes, try giving six or seven.

Even if you can't make a problem going away, being present can mean the world to someone who needs your presence.

Today I sat in a chair next to a person who had to make a difficult phone call. I did nothing but sit.

But I did everything the person needed from me.

SEPTEMBER 1, 2020

Be kind: Plant for the future.

Today I interviewed a teen who spent the pandemic learning how to garden. He built himself beds, grew an abundance of fruits and vegetables, and is learning how to build his own greenhouse.

Someday, this pandemic will end. Be kind to your future self. Build something today for tomorrow.

I'm currently writing a few books. What's your project?

SEPTEMBER 2, 2020

Be kind: Don't pour new wine into old wineskins.

Tonight at WriteOn Joliet, virtual edition again and still, we had an improv night.

This meant, someone opened a random scene, and we interacted as if we were a character from one of our books.

I chose a character that was candid, crass, and often rude.

My kids, knowing I was in the meeting, were concerned at the shouts coming from behind my door.

It was a hilarious good time and one we might never had invented if we were not holding virtual meetings over video chat.

SEPTEMBER 3, 2020

Be kind: Reach out and write someone.

Brighten someone's day with a handwritten note from you.

I have never met a person who doesn't like receiving them.

Such a person may exist. If you know one, choose someone else.

SEPTEMBER 4, 2020

Be kind: When someone you love shuts you out, stay out.

Loving someone means honoring that person's desire to stay away from us.

Demanding to fix broken relationships is often the unkind thing to do, to them, to you.

Resist the urge.

Be kind: Fix someone else's problem.

Today a family member who doesn't like me had a life or death type of problem.

I was asked to help.

And I did, with no hesitation.

As the Bible says, "If you love those who love you, what credit is that to you? Even sinners love those who love them. And if you do good to those who are good to you, what credit is that to you? Even sinners do that. And if you lend to those from whom you expect repayment, what credit is that to you? Even sinners lend to sinners, expecting to be repaid in full. But love your enemies, do good to them, and lend to them without expecting to get anything back. Then your reward will be great, and you will be children of the Most High, because he is kind to the ungrateful and wicked. Be merciful, just as your Father is merciful." Luke 6:32-36

These precepts are not just precepts for Christians. It's a good way to live for anybody.

Although for the record, it is a lot easier to love those who love us.

Be kind: Step out of your comfort zone and into someone else's.

One of my sons who's lived in poverty for many years landed a higher paying job this year and rented a really nice ranch house this past week for himself and his family.

Of course, we're in the middle of a pandemic.

But we masked up, stayed six feet apart, and went for a tour of the house.

We stayed less than two hours and about half of that time was spent outside.

And we hope the guidelines for reducing transmission are correct.

My grandchildren were thrilled to see me, by the way.

SEPTEMBER 7, 2020

Be kind: Share words.

I typically spend Labor Day working. To me, using my skills for the benefit of another is a great day to celebrate a day dedicated to labor.

Yesterday was the first Labor Day in decades where I wasn't scheduled to work. So I finished editing a poetry book for a client.

Yes, I'd had a challenging weekend, and I could have used the downtime.

But my client has her own challenges, hopes, aspirations, and goals.

So today, I used my skills to help meet those for her.

SEPTEMBER 8, 2020

Be kind: Give the gift of family history.

Today for my son Timothy's thirtieth birthday present, I sent him links to Yama Farms in New York.

He doesn't know much about Yama Farms – yet.

But Yama Farms is important in our family's genealogy. And Timothy likes history.

During some downtime, the links will be there waiting for him.

I hope he enjoys exploring and discovering.

Timothy is the type of person who appreciates history of all kind, especially family history.

He isn't the type of person who wants, or expects, expensive presents, although he certainly appreciates them. Rather, he is the type of man who will always go the extra mile for another, even if he grumbles about it at first. Seriously. Ask him to go one mile, he'll always go two.

He's a careful spender, especially when it comes to expensive purchases, such as cell phones and vehicles. He will research his options for months and then ensures he gets the most for his money.

Just so you know.

SEPTEMBER 9, 2020

Be kind: Give the gift of their personal history.

People love when others recall positive moments in their lives that were also positive moments in yours.

Share them: by phone, text, letter.

What did someone do for you a long time ago that's a great memory in your life?

SEPTEMBER 10, 2020

Be kind. Let people share their stories and give them time to tell it.

Today I interviewed a person who survived a serious "widow maker" heart attack.

This person shared the story in an interesting, but lengthy and detailed, way. And I provided two ears and quick fingers to catch all the information.

Sometimes people process as they talk. Sometimes they need to be heard.

Now I have deadlines, of course. And at some point, if an interview goes quite a long time, I do have to wrap it up.

But I have quite a bit of leeway from here to there. I don't always need to be impatient and quick to end the conversation. Perhaps if I'd had such an experience, I'd share it the same way.

And while I'm being patient, I can be thankful I'm healthy enough to listen, type, and write.

SEPTEMBER 11, 2020

Be kind: Meet a real need.

One of my sons takes a medicine that he must take every day. In fact, if he runs out, or if the doctor is slow to submit a refill to the pharmacy, the pharmacy must fill an emergency dose.

After a few days of emergency dosages, with my son getting nowhere with calls back to the doctor's receptionist, I stopped my work in the middle of the afternoon, masked up, and headed over.

As soon as I charged into the office, the receptionist saw me and said, "I was just faxing it in. Unless you want me to call it in."

I opted for the call. And I waited until the call had ended, and I had a pickup time for that medicine later today for my son.

It took me less than half an hour on a busy day to do. But it was an excellent use of my time.

SEPTEMBER 12, 2020

Be kind: Be selfish with your time but not too selfish.

Saturdays is my fiction writing day, but sometimes I also work on that day, either because I'm scheduled to work it or because that's the best time to connect with story sources.

Most of the time, the day remains sacred. But a despotic attitude isn't the best one.

So, yes, I'm territorial with that time because I need a large chunk of it to focus on the storyline, which I just don't have during the week.

But sometimes, I need to give a little.

And when I do, I often find another opportunity opens up.

That said, remember to, overall, guard the time you need for yourself.

Not everyone who wants it has your best interests in mind.

You matter, too.

SEPTEMBER 13, 2020

Be kind: You erred? Forgive yourself

Today I sent out an editing contract with the wrong name at the bottom. Fortunately, the client caught the error.

Well, it's been an extremely challenging week. But honestly, I could have made the same mistake if it had been a good week. Errors happen sometimes.

I could relentlessly beat myself up for it. I mean, it's a contract for an editing job editing job with an editing error.

Or I can recognize the error, apologize, resolve to do better, forgive myself, send the correct information, and move forward.

Brooding almost ensures I'll make more mistakes, while making myself miserable in the process.

And it's not really the example I'd like other writers to follow.

And if they did – well, that's one terrible way to multiply one mistake.

SEPTEMBER 14, 2020

Be kind: Learn how to carry your cross.

Today in the Orthodox Church, we celebrate the finding of Christ's cross.

Regardless of the faith we practice, all of us have burdens.
Do we carry them with grace?
Do we bury them in the ground and refuse to address them?
Do we moan and grumble about the unfairness of it all?
Do we help carry the burdens of others?
Thoughtful questions, indeed.

SEPTEMBER 15, 2020

Be kind: Give the gift of wonder.

This past spring, we printed out a few of our favorite home-schooling science experiments, bought all the ingredients, portioned them out, packaged them up, and delivered to several grandchildren with birthdays close together.

I just learned that they enjoyed them and that they came in very handy for their busy moms, who are adjusting to the ropes of remote learning as they go.

One year for Old Calendar Christmas (our entire family Christmas), I showed the grandkids how to make bread from scratch and then shape their portions into bears, which they decorated and ate.

Not as "cool" as gift cards to their favorite video games.

But the time they spent engaged with each other may foster memories that will last longer than their enjoyment of the video games.

SEPTEMBER 16, 2020

Be kind: Let others shine.

Tonight I brought something to read at WriteOn Joliet.

And tonight I stepped back from reading it – not for reasons of false humility, etc.

But because I'm fortunate enough to write in an industry where people read my work.

Not all writers are that fortunate for now. But I can help provide sets of ears and people who will offer feedback.

That's really all most writers ultimately want: to be heard and appreciated.

SEPTEMBER 17, 2020

Be kind: Develop another's potential.

While Rebekah is unemployed, she is keeping busy adding to her skillset. Of course, I'm encouraging her, but encouragement alone doesn't pay the bills or bring inner satisfaction.

So in addition to offering planet of "rah-rahs" I also actively seek out ways she might be able to use those skills.

True, people might need to hear "I believe in you" to advance to the next opportunity.

Others simply need solid job leads.

Bolstering isn't a one-size-fits-all activity. But tailoring the development to the need is a great day to support someone you love.

Be kind: Connect someone who needs help with someone who can help.

Tonight I received a call from someone who found injured wildlife asking if I knew someone who could help. And I did.

That person didn't know what to do. But I knew someone who did.

And now two tiny, hungry, rain-soaked, orphaned mammals get to grow up and life.

SEPTEMBER 19, 2020

Be kind: Weed out condescension.

When my three younger kids were working and attending college, I did most of the chores so they could concentrate fully on these two tasks.

But that doesn't meant they never did housework. Often, when Rebekah helped out, she would say she did it "for me."

"I emptied the dishwasher for you," she'd say or "I started the towels for you."

I'd then remind her that she did it for all of us, including herself. We all used the dishes and the towels.

Since she's been out of work, Rebekah voluntarily took over the housework, insisting it made her feel "useful."

But that doesn't make her our maid. From time to time, I jump in to prove that point.

Today, I almost told her that I'd emptied the dishwasher "for her."

I learned two things. One, the phrase is easy to slip from our lips.

Two, I needed to be reminded of the great service she's doing for all of us and not to take it for granted.

SEPTEMBER 20, 2020

Be kind: Walk away when someone is in a mood.

Rebekah gets anxious when she is stretching her skills.

Today she was trying some new recipes and snapped at me when I came down to make myself a snack.

I could have told her off. I could have chastised her disrespect. I could have made her feel guilty and caused her to blow up some more.

Instead, I took my plate and went back upstairs to work.

And now, I can scarcely remember what she said. Plus, I know that, whatever it was, she didn't mean it.

Walking away quickly restored serenity for both of us.

Not every opposition should be a fight to the death.

SEPTEMBER 21, 2020

Be kind: Let something go.

I didn't meet a goal for this month, and the month is nearly done.

But I had a lot of goals to meet. And we can't always make them all.

Sometimes, it's kinder to move the goal down the list and move on.

SEPTEMBER 22, 2020

Be kind: Revel in seasons.

As much as I dislike seeing summer slip away, especially since I missed most of summer for years in a row, I can also immerse myself into the crisp, cool air and crisp, colorful leaves of autumn.

It means I can enjoy these blessings without suffering from asthma, thanks to a medication combination that works for me.

Swimming and boating in fresh water and digging one's toes into the warm sand are magical for me.

But so are cool nights and warm fires.

SEPTEMBER 23, 2020

Be kind: Face your fears.

I am a medically anxious person and so is Rebekah.

Today on our walk, we called our primary care physical and made appointments for our physicals.

We also made appointments with our endocrinologist.

None of this makes the fear go away. In fact, I can feel the adrenalin just by typing these words.

No matter how well we care for our bodies, they will not run smoothly all the time.

But one way to guarantee they will break down more often is to refuse to perform the maintenance checks and catch the inevitable early.

Plus, we looked fear in the eye and made the right move anyway.

Isn't that a good use of time?

SEPTEMBER 24, 2020

Be kind: Remember those in prison.

We used to write letters to a member of our church who served time (more than once) for drug possession. He has since died.

We prayed for a step sister-in-law who served time for reckless homicide. She has since been released.

But some people are bound by the prison of their thoughts, needs, desires, attitudes, life circumstances.

Write letters of encouragement to them, too.

Pray for them, too.

SEPTEMBER 25, 2020

Be kind: Give someone leeway, especially when that person is being tested.

If someone is stressed and under pressure, try to give some leeway for snappish moods.

You don't have to tolerate downright disrespect, of course.

But be gentle when countering it, especially if the person is already feeling low.

Be kind: Show up

Today on my lone free day this week, I covered a story about a local church giving away over $1,000 in free gas.

And then I attended a book signing of a good acquaintance and former student. And then I attended a virtual funeral of someone I'd covered in stories with the goal of getting him closer to a kidney donor, a person who'd found inspiration in my past health experiences.

It's hard to give up free time when free time is slim. And I'm not going to say something as cliché as I gained more than I gave: as if the free gas, writing accomplishments of a local writer, and the funeral of a local resident was about me.

But today, I did do the decent human thing of showing up where I was required to be. I provided support with my presence. And I didn't even grumble.

Yes, of course, I felt good about it and would have felt terrible if I hadn't.

But the kindness wasn't for me. It was for them. And I gave it.

SEPTEMBER 27, 2020

Be kind: Help a stranger

Tonight I connected with someone I have never met because this person might have an undiagnosed pheochromocytoma.

I reached out after this person liked one of my blogs that referenced "pheochromocytoma" after I'd posted it on social media.

It sure felt good to bring some comfort and hope to a person who was a kid when I was going through it.

I used to wonder why God lets us go through these things. The general response is "so we can help someone else," blah, blah.

But God, being God, doesn't need our "help."

Tonight, however, provided fresh insight. If God just erases all problems, we never get to feel the joy of being sent my God to share that comfort and hope to another.

God would get the joy. We'd just be watching TV.

SEPTEMBER 28, 2020

Be kind: Embrace Monday

Many people greet Monday with, "Ugh, Monday."

How about, "Welcome, Monday. What new opportunities might we explore together?"

Yeah, I definitely need to work on this one. But it's a good thought, isn't it?

Be kind: Spotlight a young person's good qualities

Recently a local teen stepped far out of her comfort zone to raise money for a classmate who needs an adaptive van.

Yes, I wrote about it.

It isn't the type of story that will go viral. But it is the type of story that will help two teens: the one who needs the van and the one who may continue doing good over and over again for decades to come, just because someone took the time to notice and affirm long after the present generation of grownups are gone.

Be kind: Share three talents of loved ones with others.

Because this book is only nine months long, I will share three talents for each of my last two children: Rebekah Anne and Daniel John.

Rebekah's birthday is January 7, and she's outstanding at navigating technology. She can understand new skills very quickly and can monitor my learning with one eye on her phone. It's been great working at home with her across the hall. If I run into any technology rut, she can tow me out in mere seconds.

She is aware of minute needs of people in her life. Rebekah regularly checks my clothes for repair or the need for dry cleaning. She regular checks the cupboards and closets to ensure we don't run out of essential items during a pandemic (and we haven't).

Rebekah is also very brave. She recently went through hours of neuropsychological testing, and the tester is anticipating an autism diagnosis. Somehow, Rebekah has dealt with this disability by herself her entire life. That, coupled with her dyslexia, has made her anxious in many situations. We are hoping the light is at the end of the tunnel for her.

Daniel, too, has overcome many challenging health situations in his life and is currently working in management in a very good job with an incredible future.

His birthday is October 11.

Daniel is the most patient, even-tempered of all my children. It takes a great deal to rile him and even that less than once a year.

He routinely assumes extra tasks to help another.

He has traditional, old-fashioned values. Think of Ward Cleaver. Yet, he's a single twenty-four-year-old that doesn't drink, doesn't smoke, and has gone to work, home, and the store all through the pandemic. Period.

www.ingramcontent.com/pod-product-compliance
Lightning Source LLC
Chambersburg PA
CBHW030915090426
42737CB00007B/206